W9-CFK-748

Rock 'n' Roll Dances of the 1950s

Rock 'n' Roll Dances of the 1950s

Lisa Jo Sagolla

The American Dance Floor
Ralph G. Giordano, Series Editor

 GREENWOOD

AN IMPRINT OF ABC-CLIO, LLC
Santa Barbara, California • Denver, Colorado • Oxford, England

Copyright 2011 by Lisa Jo Sagolla

All rights reserved. No part of this publication may be reproduced, stored in a retrieval system, or transmitted, in any form or by any means, electronic, mechanical, photocopying, recording, or otherwise, except for the inclusion of brief quotations in a review, without prior permission in writing from the publisher.

Library of Congress Cataloging-in-Publication Data

Sagolla, Lisa Jo.
 Rock 'n' roll dances of the 1950s / Lisa Jo Sagolla.
     p. cm. — (The American dance floor)
 Includes bibliographical references and index.
 ISBN 978-0-313-36556-0 (hardback) — ISBN 978-0-313-36557-7 (ebook)   1. Rock and roll dancing—United States—History.   I. Title.
 GV1796.R6S24   2011
 793.3'3—dc23   2011018831

ISBN: 978-0-313-36556-0
EISBN: 978-0-313-36557-7

15 14 13 12 11   1 2 3 4 5

This book is also available on the World Wide Web as an eBook.
Visit www.abc-clio.com for details.

Greenwood
An Imprint of ABC-CLIO, LLC

ABC-CLIO, LLC
130 Cremona Drive, P.O. Box 1911
Santa Barbara, California 93116-1911

This book is printed on acid-free paper ∞

Manufactured in the United States of America

To Richard Pirodsky

Contents

Series Foreword

From the Lindy hop to hip hop, dance has helped define American life and culture. In good times and bad, people have turned to dance to escape their troubles, get out, and have a good time. From high school proms to weddings and other occasions, dance creates some of our most memorable personal moments. It is also big business, with schools, competitions, and dance halls bringing in people and their dollars each year. And as America has changed, so, too, has dance. The story of dance is very much the story of America. Dance routines are featured in movies, television, and videos; dance styles and techniques reflect shifting values and attitudes toward relationships; and dance performers and their costumes reveal changing thoughts about race, class, gender, and other topics. Written for students and general readers, The American Dance Floor series covers the history of social dancing in America.

Each volume in the series looks at a particular type of dance such as swing, disco, Latin, folk dancing, hip hop, ballroom, and country & western. Written in an engaging manner, each book tells the story of a particular dance form and places it in its historical, social, and cultural context. Thus each title helps the reader learn not only about a particular dance form, but also about social change. The volumes are fully documented, and each contains a bibliography of print and electronic resources for further reading.

Introduction

Dancing to rock 'n' roll music was an expressive, emblematic, often defiant, and profoundly defining act for the teenagers of 1950s America. However, unlike the 1960s, the 1950s did not yield any vast variety of new rock 'n' roll dances. Fifties teens could sometimes be seen doing freshly invented dances, such as the Stroll, the Hand Jive, the Bop, the Slop, the Madison, and the Twist. But the dance most commonly performed to 1950s rock 'n' roll was the Jitterbug, that same Swing dance the teens' parents had done throughout the '30s and '40s. The Swing moves were simply adapted to the rock 'n' roll beat. Yet, while they may have been dancing the same steps as their parents, how they danced, where they danced, when they danced, and why they danced made the Jitterbugging of '50s teens a truly original event: a vivid reflection of the bracing cultural trends then shaping American life.

The 1950s was an era marked by simmering tensions born out of contradictions between the traditional values of those in power and the new ideas of young innovators who were instigating changes in social relations, technology, business, the arts, and entertainment. The decade is often called the Eisenhower Era, after Dwight David Eisenhower, who served as the nation's president from 1953 to 1961, yet was born in 1890. Throughout the 1950s, most of the country's leaders had, like Eisenhower, come of age in early 20th-century America and were driven by a vision of the nation reminiscent of their youth.[1]

Meanwhile, America's flourishing post-war economy was spurring all kinds of cutting-edge developments that were radically altering what it meant to be an American. The mass migration of African

Americans to northern cities following World War II spawned a fascination with urban black culture. There was an increased and potent
impact of black culture on American life, notably in sports and in the
visual, dramatic, literary, and musical arts. A 1954 Supreme Court decision outlawing school segregation incited dramatic changes in social
relations between the races.

Inventive technological advancements generated an array of new
products that Americans rushed out to buy: homes in the suburbs,
fancy cars, fast food, household appliances, and television sets. Consumer spending was abundant as the population turned away from
earlier, Puritan-inspired and Great Depression–influenced ideas of restraint. A new generation arose, which had more money than its prede-
cessor, freer spending habits, and a confidence in prolonged prosperity.
With little interest in the strict moral codes or otherwise conservative
behavior of their parents, the teenagers of the 1950s emerged as an
economically significant demographic whose new tastes and interests
were beginning to exert strong influence on American business, particularly in the music and entertainment industries.[2]

But underlying the optimism of the Fifties youth was a constant
struggle to move forward in an era when power was still largely in the
hands of an older order. Though the decade is commonly remembered
as a quiet, conformist period, that is largely because of the media's
depictions of happy Fifties families, such as in the popular television
show *The Adventures of Ozzie and Harriet*. In reality, the 1950s was a period of great social stress. It was via the revolutionary invention of rock
'n' roll music and the liberating dancing that was performed to it that
the pressure of the 1950s exploded. The rock 'n' roll dancing of the era,
therefore, can function as a wide-angle lens, offering an animated view
of the decade's overall cultural climate.

The emergence of the younger generation as a new and influential
social group was signaled loudly and clearly by the teens' adoption of
rock 'n' roll as a defining badge, which branded them as a generation
distinctly separate from their parents. When they got up and moved
to "their" music, the teens were proclaiming their independence, in defiance of the musical tastes, social attitudes, and cultural behaviors of
adult society. While publicly embodying the beat of rock 'n' roll—a
musical genre born out of a blending of black and white styles—the
teens of the '50s were also acting out their support of racial integration,
at the same time that issues of school desegregation and civil rights

were charging onto the nation's political forefront. The conflicts and controversies sparked by adults' reactions to the Jitterbugging teens unveiled the deep-rooted racial prejudices harbored by many Americans of the time, as well as the conservative sexual innocence that has come to be associated with the era.

Many adults violently objected to what they perceived as rock 'n' roll's vulgar qualities: its hard-driving beat; the sexual innuendos in the song lyrics; its roots in African-American rhythm and blues, then referred to as "race" music; and the association between rock 'n' roll and juvenile delinquency being put forth by Hollywood films. Parents were horrified enough by their teens' interest in listening to rock 'n' roll. But when their kids began to dance to the music, that was even more frightening. In adults' eyes, as teens moved to the rock 'n' roll beat, it was as if the dancers' young bodies were invaded by the vulgar sounds, their youthful physicality becoming a very visceral expression of all of the music's objectionable connotations.

In addition to signifying an act of adolescent rebellion and a thwarting of social conventions, dancing to rock 'n' roll in the 1950s also illustrated how economic factors stemming from the culture's latest technological developments contributed to teens' newfound independence. It was in the mid-1950s that transistor radios first became available to the general public, making it easier for teens to go off alone and listen to music of their own choosing. They were less likely to have to sit around the family radio in the living room and submit to their parents' programming tastes.[3] Without little portable radios, rock 'n' roll would surely not have taken off as speedily as it did. As radio stations popularized the latest rock 'n' roll songs, the teenagers ran out to buy them on 45 rpm singles, a new, inexpensive record format that made the disks affordable for the teens, who then used the records to provide soundtracks for their social dance parties.

The extensive role played by television, most notably the famed teen dance program *American Bandstand,* in the dissemination of rock 'n' roll dance styles shows yet another way in which this dancing provides a lively vantage from which to observe the larger cultural phenomena of the times. With its real-life participants and its soap opera–like emphasis on their personal lives, *American Bandstand* can be considered a forerunner of the reality shows that became a staple of television programming around the turn of the 21st century. Although *American Bandstand* included appearances by popular rock 'n' roll performers of the day, the program's tremendous success in the 1950s relied essentially on viewers' fascination with watching ordinary teenagers in the act of dancing. The 1950s was a landmark era in the history of television and is often referred to as the medium's "Golden Age." *American Bandstand*'s pioneering role in television history (it can be seen as a precursor to music videos as well as reality TV) is yet another feature of the cultural climate of the '50s that is unearthed through the study of the era's rock 'n' roll dancing.

Setting the stage with an opening chapter tracing the explosive birth of rock 'n' roll music, this book explores the many ways in which Fifties rock 'n' roll dancing mirrors critical artistic, social, and political aspects of the decade. The book includes specific descriptions of the steps, rhythms, and other choreographic characteristics of each of the dances executed to rock 'n' roll music during the 1950s. However, the main purpose of this book is to show how it is not knowledge of the dances themselves, but an understanding of what the execution of those dances represented that constitutes the real value of studying the topic. Such understanding can prove beneficial to almost anyone interested in learning more about life in America during the 1950s.

The book's second and third chapters, therefore, introduce Fifties rock 'n' roll dances by situating them firmly within discussions of such social-history topics as the emerging youth culture, changing racial relationships, and the increasing influence of television on many facets of American society. Chapter 4 brings the book's investigation of the Fifties dances to a close with the extraordinary story of the Twist, a dance that not only reflected the cultural climate of the late '50s, but foreshadowed much of what was to come in the 1960s.

Though the subject of this book is delineated as rock 'n' roll dancing of the 1950s, its scope does not correspond neatly to the historical period from 1951 to 1960. Instead, as rock 'n' roll music did not emerge until 1954, the book's treatment of Fifties rock 'n' roll dancing starts from that date and extends to 1963, which was when the popularity of the Twist, the final rock 'n' roll dance invented in the 1950s, waned.

While this book is designed primarily to serve students of American social dance and those looking to find new ways of examining the history of the 1950s, it may also be useful to readers seeking to learn more about the legacy of that decade and its impact on future generations. The book's final chapter focuses on the presence of rock 'n' roll dancing in the Fifties nostalgia movement that began at the end of the 1960s, became a driving force in the entertainment industries and popular culture of the Seventies, and inspired the periodic resurfacing of '50s rock 'n' roll in films, Broadway shows, and TV programs of the next 30 years.

The most important aspect of dancing to rock 'n' roll in any era, however, is the skintight relationship that has always existed between the music and the dance movements. It is impossible to overestimate the importance of the music to anything and everything the rock 'n' roll dancer does. The music is the rocket fuel that propels the dancing, and that music–movement relationship is not only unbreakable, but also irresistible. Many claim that it is impossible *not* to dance to rock 'n' roll music.

Therefore, any serious investigation of rock 'n' roll dancing must begin with an understanding of rock 'n' roll music, that incendiary art form that burst onto America's popular music scene in the mid-1950s. Where did rock 'n' roll come from? Who invented it? And what made it such an unconquerable catalyst for social dancing?

1

The Detonation of
Rock 'n' Roll Music

An electrifying cultural force that launched with supersonic speed and brawn in the mid-1950s, rock 'n' roll music is a hybrid composed of elements from three strands of American music: pop, country and western, and rhythm and blues. All three were adult-oriented forms, popular during the early 1950s.

Pop music, sporting a slick, professional sound, was rooted in the Broadway show tunes, romantic ballads, and fun novelty songs of New York's Tin Pan Alley. As a musical term, Tin Pan Alley refers not only to the group of music publishers and songwriters who drove American popular music throughout the first half of the 20th century, but also to the style of music they produced: songs with melodic appeal, witty lyrics, and accessibility.[1] The pop music industry of the 1950s was controlled by an older generation of adults whose interests ran counter to the decade's burgeoning youth culture. Hence, the pop songs of the day reflected the tastes of those who had been born in the early 20th century. Having lived through the Great Depression of the 1930s and then World War II, they had developed escapist notions of musical entertainment, and enjoyed pleasant, soothing songs that served to relieve tension, rather than instigate excessive emotional turbulence.

Country and western music came primarily from the South and Southwest, often featured the steel guitar, traditionally scorned the use of drums, and was predominantly associated with poor and working-class white listeners.[2] The name "country and western" was introduced in 1949 by *Billboard*, the music industry's leading trade publication, to replace the term "hillbilly music." The roots of the "country" element of country and western music are in the traditional songs of Appalachia, which derive from the folk music brought to that region by early American settlers from the British Isles. The "western" strand has its origins in the cowboy songs of the American Southwest and the blend of country and jazz dance-hall music that came to be known as "western swing."

Rhythm and blues, tagged "race" music in the 1920s, was performed mainly by and for African Americans. In 1949, looking for a less-offensive name for the recordings then classified as "race records," *Billboard* coined the term "rhythm and blues" to refer to any black popular music of the day that wasn't jazz or gospel. Rhythm and blues was typically characterized by an emphatic dance rhythm, a harsh singing style, little emphasis on melody, loud volume, and emotional excitement.[3]

The rhythm and blues music of the early 1950s could be loosely categorized into three strains: jump blues, the music of the blues shouters, and doo-wop. Jump blues is an up-tempo form, strongly influenced by the propulsive jazz piano style known as boogie-woogie. Generally performed by small combos of piano, bass, drums, and horns, jump blues is considered to be reflective of a northern, urban sensibility. The blues shouters were loud singers, usually male, who shouted to be heard over the band, and were often associated with the singing of sexually explicit, sometimes vulgar or misogynistic, lyrics.[4] The term "doo-wop" refers to a smooth style of consonant, close-harmony group singing, reminiscent of the late 19th-century barbershop quartet sound, and rooted in African-American gospel music. Songs by doo-wop groups, composed of usually four or five singers, would create an important sub-genre of Fifties rock 'n' roll music, although it was not until the early 1960s that the term "doo-wop" came into popular usage as a descriptor of their singing style. Whereas the other forms of rock 'n' roll mirrored the rebellious spirit of adolescents, the gentler doo-wop music captured the angst and loneliness commonly experienced by young teens.

It was not uncommon for middle-class African Americans in the early 1950s to shun rhythm and blues, much of which, with its suggestive lyrics and crude sensibilities, they felt perpetuated a negative stereotype of blacks. As a musical expression of the African-American experience, instead of the "disreputable" rhythm and blues, they preferred the more morally respectable gospel music or the sophisticated jazz of the day. The main difference between rhythm and blues and the jazz of this period lies in the presence or absence of a dance beat. The distinctive characteristic of all the rhythm and blues styles was the strong presence of a dance rhythm, whereas post-war jazz was rarely intended as dance music.

Another characteristic that distinguished rhythm and blues from jazz, and was clearly carried over into rock 'n' roll, was the dominance of the vocal soloist. In rhythm and blues, a solo singer typically expressed his or her own feelings and personality. The band was often relegated to the role of keeping the beat going and the volume up. In jazz, on the other hand, the focus was on complex interplay among a group of musicians and deeper explorations of melody and harmony. From the rhythm and blues singers of the early '50s, with their ferocious personas and individualized forms of expressivity, can be traced the ancestral roots of the "rock star."

Though rock 'n' roll drew from three different musical genres, it did so in unequal proportions. While it borrowed polished vocal stylings characteristic of pop music, and took rural flavorings from country and western, the essential component of early rock 'n' roll music is rhythm and blues.

When the term "rock 'n' roll" was first introduced as a description of a musical form, it referred directly to rhythm and blues. However, the term emerged at the exact time when that music was being heavily marketed to teenage fans, both black and white. The music's producers and promoters were working to expand its listenership beyond its traditional niche audience of African Americans. It was while widening its appeal that rhythm and blues began to absorb the characteristics from other musical genres that led to its transformation into the new mongrel rock 'n' roll.[5]

Economic Factors

The invention and take-off of rock 'n' roll music are inextricably linked to the emergence in the 1950s of a new adolescent culture, a population armed with significant buying power and rebellious spirit. The new musical form not only mirrored adolescence in its emotional volatility and authority-defying attitudes, but the subject matter of most rock 'n' roll songs was aimed directly at topics of teenage interest, such as romantic crushes, school, going to dances, and parental discipline.

While many adults harbored distaste for rock 'n' roll because of its association with adolescent rebellion, and others' objections to it were grounded in the bi-racial make-up of the music, serious anti-rock 'n' roll sentiments also stemmed from economic concerns within the entertainment industry. Not everyone in the music business stood to gain from the sensational success of the new musical genre. The already-declining sheet music sector, for example, was hurt by the speed at which rock 'n' roll hits came and went. And the livelihood of established singers, instrumentalists, arrangers, orchestrators, copyists, and conductors whose aesthetics were firmly rooted in pre–rock 'n' roll styles were threatened.[6]

As the popularity of rock 'n' roll records skyrocketed with shocking speed, the major recording companies suddenly found their records facing competition for spots on the hit charts from records produced by smaller, independent labels. The major labels did not immediately devote significant resources to the production of rock 'n' roll music, as it was initially thought to be a passing fad. It was the independent companies, which had specialized mainly in ethnic folk music and rhythm and blues, that more readily embraced and cultivated the recordings of the early rock 'n' roll artists.

The American Society of Composers, Authors, and Publishers (ASCAP), the era's predominant music licensing organization, also had much to lose as a consequence of the meteoric rise of rock 'n' roll. It was ASCAP that controlled the licensing of songs' performance rights to broadcasting outlets, primarily radio. But in 1939, an association of radio stations had set up a rival organization, Broadcast Music Incorporated (BMI), which represented many of the songwriters and publishers neglected by ASCAP. These included a lot of the country and western and rhythm and blues artists whose music, thanks to the rock 'n' roll fusions, was suddenly growing in popularity.[7]

Radio Fuels the Fire

One sector of the music industry that enthusiastically welcomed the arrival of rock 'n' roll, however, was radio, for which the new music became a savior from the potentially devastating impact of television.

The new medium of television, with its added visual component, was demonstrating that it could more effectively produce the kinds of comedy, drama, and variety-show programming that radio had offered. And by the 1950s, television sets were becoming inexpensive enough that more households than ever before could afford one. In 1950, there was a television set in only 9 percent of American homes. Three years later, half the households in America had a TV.[8]

In the early days of rock 'n' roll, however, television was still catering primarily to an adult audience and seemed to have little interest in programming the new teen music. Reflecting the widespread adult disapproval of rock 'n' roll music, John Hammond wrote in the *New York Herald Tribune* (July 18, 1955), "Rock 'n' roll is not what might be described as respectable music. It is abhorred by music critics, scorned by the better instrumentalists, loathed by the traditional ASCAP publishers, blamed by sociologists as a contributing factor to juvenile delinquency and banned by the police in several large New England communities." But needing to somehow maintain its listenership, radio was more than happy to court the teenagers and capitalize on their desire to hear their new music. By 1956, 68 percent of the music played by radio disc jockeys in the United States was rock 'n' roll.[9]

Ironically, even though the music belongs undeniably to the teenage culture, it was an adult, the ambitious, charismatic disc jockey Alan Freed, who recognized, harnessed, and pointed the youth culture's enormous energies toward the popularization of rock 'n' roll. Freed is frequently credited with coining the term rock 'n' roll, which, it will become clear, is only a partially deserved honor.

Radio disc jockeys, by the 1950s, had become the primary promotional channels between record manufacturers and the listening public. In 1951, a Cleveland record-store owner, Leo Mintz, bought airtime on the city's radio station WJW and gave it to Freed to host a late-night rhythm and blues show. The object was for Freed, whose on-air moniker was "Moondog," to promote the sale of rhythm and blues records in what was then the seventh-largest city in the United States, with a black population of almost 130,000.[10]

Though not initially a fan of the music, Freed became convinced of rhythm and blues' potential to reach wide audiences when Mintz pointed out that the music's beat was so driving that anybody could dance to it. It was indeed its undeniably danceable beat that made rhythm and blues, and its offspring rock 'n' roll, so infectious and such a perfect complement to youthful teenage energy. By the early '50s, numerous radio stations were programming rhythm and blues in an attempt to reach a newly emerging market of black consumers who, in the post-war era, were moving from the south into northern urban areas in great numbers. Spurred in large part by the mechanization of cotton harvesting introduced in the 1930s, from 1940 to 1950, 1.25 million African Americans left the South and traveled northward.[11]

But while other disc jockeys were playing rhythm and blues music, Freed was unique in that he was aiming to build a white audience for it. And that audience was composed largely of teenagers.[12]

Well aware that the sale of pop records was dependent on the artists making public appearances, Freed branched out into concert presenting and organized highly successful concert events in Ohio that allowed teens to hear and dance to the most popular rhythm and blues artists of the day. As his radio show continued to grow in popularity it was picked up, in 1953, by WNJR in Newark, New Jersey, where Freed then organized an astoundingly well-attended dance. Thousands of teens had to be turned away. Ironically, the dance was so crowded that dancing proved impossible. Soon after, Freed was hired to host a radio show on WINS in New York City. It was via that program, which debuted in 1954, that a surge of white teens discovered and fell in love with rhythm and blues.[13]

As the music gained popularity among white youth, it began to arouse much derisive criticism. While conservative adults seemed genuinely offended by its smutty lyrics and some African Americans were ashamed of its primitive sensibilities, Freed felt that many of the complaints railed against rhythm and blues had little to do with aesthetics and everything to do with economics. For example, ASCAP's critical comments about the music could be seen to stem from the fact that the organization's long-standing monopoly on pop song licensing fees was being cut into by the upstart BMI.[14]

When Freed moved his radio program to New York, he was no longer allowed to use the name "Moondog" (a visually impaired street musician, Louis "Moondog" Hardin, claimed Freed had stolen the name from him), so Freed changed the title of his show from "The Moondog House" to "The Rock 'n' Roll Party." He was cautioned against using the term "rock 'n' roll," as it was widely considered a black euphemism for sexual intercourse. In 1920s "race" music, the words "rock" and "roll" had been used separately to refer to sex, but by the '30s and

Alan Freed, the disc jockey and concert producer who sparked the popularization of rock 'n' roll. (Photo by Hulton Archive/Getty Images)

'40s, "rock and roll" had come to refer to a rhythmic sensuality contained in the era's swing music. In the 1934 film *Transatlantic Merry-Go-Round*, the vocal trio The Boswell Sisters sang "Rock and Roll," a song about a type of Swing dancing. Some rhythm and blues songs of the early 1950s, however, made use of variations of the words "rocking" and "rolling" as sexual innuendos.[15] But whatever its connotations or origins, the term "rock 'n' roll" quickly came to mean the kind of music being heard on Freed's radio show. And record companies soon started using the term as the name of a category of music aimed at America's youth.

While it is virtually impossible to pinpoint exactly when, by whom, or in what song the musical fusion of rock 'n' roll was first heard, the cover version of "Rock Around the Clock," released on May 10, 1954, by Bill Haley & His Comets is often heralded as the start of the rock 'n' roll phenomenon.

"Cover" is a term used to describe a recording of a song made by an artist other than the one who originally recorded it. Covers are generally made with the intention of allowing a song to be marketed to an audience that the original version could not or would not reach. White artists' bowdlerized cover versions of songs originally recorded by black performers played a big role in the early history of rock 'n' roll, when it was thought that the distinctively "black" vocal sounds or naughty lyrics would compromise the music's marketability to audiences outside the African-American community. While the sanitized cover version of a song often sold much better than the original, sometimes a cover would spark listeners' interest in hearing the song's original version, which would then become a hit record. Many rock 'n' roll fans and music critics have come to denounce, and even deplore, the practice of covering for what they see as its artistic inauthenticity and blatant commercial intentions.

One of the most famous cover stories in rock 'n' roll lore involves the song "Ain't That a Shame." Written by the African-American pioneering rock 'n' roll artist Antoine "Fats" Domino and Dave Bartholomew, the song was originally recorded by Domino in the spring of 1955. A blander cover version was recorded that summer by the squeaky-clean, white pop singer Pat Boone. Boone's cover was a huge hit and wound up generating enormous interest in Domino's original recording, which then went on to sell even more copies than Boone's cover. Before recording the song, Boone wanted to "clean up" the title lyric by altering it to the more grammatically correct "Isn't That a Shame," fearing his more educated, white, upper-middle-class audiences might be put off by the word "ain't."[16] Though he was eventually dissuaded from making that alteration, the title lyric was changed from the original "Ain't It a Shame" to "Ain't That a Shame." It has been speculated that the reason the word "it" was changed to "that" was because in the natural carry-over of consonant sounds that occurs when singing, the original wording might cause listeners to inadvertently hear the word "tit."

The breakthrough cover version of "Rock Around the Clock" is a clear representation of the merging of the three musical strands that formed rock 'n' roll. Originally recorded by Sonny Dae and His Knights, "Rock Around the Clock" was written by Tin Pan Alley songwriter Max C. Freedman and James E. Myers (under the pseudonym Jimmy De Knight). But when Haley, a western singer-guitarist (once a cowboy yodeler), recorded "Rock Around the Clock," he added a strong rhythm and blues dance beat and essentially transformed the song into a jump blues number. The original recording was not a big hit, nor was Haley's when it was initially released in 1954. But thanks to its inclusion the following year in a watershed Hollywood movie, *Blackboard Jungle* (1955), Haley's "Rock Around the Clock" became astoundingly popular. It was the first rock 'n' roll record to hit No. 1 on the *Billboard* pop charts, a position it held on to for eight weeks.

Haley had previously had a hit with his 1953 recording of "Crazy Man, Crazy." Some cite this record as the start of rock 'n' roll because it demonstrated how Haley was beginning to inject his country and western music with a rhythm and blues beat. However, with its prominent placement in *Blackboard Jungle*, "Rock Around the Clock" solidified the relationship between the new rock 'n' roll sound and the defiant attitudes of '50s teens. It is for this reason that "Rock Around the Clock" is commonly considered the birth announcement of rock 'n' roll.

Hollywood Fans the Flames

With films such as *The Wild One* (1953) and *Rebel Without a Cause* (1955), Hollywood had already begun making headway into the teenage market. Marlon Brando's iconic portrayal of the leader of a motorcycle gang in *The Wild One* put a potently charismatic face on rebellious behavior. And in *Rebel Without a Cause*, heartthrob James Dean's powerful performance as a troubled youth made the bravado of the disobedient teenager downright alluring. Yet, while those movies depicted generational conflict and featured boldly defiant young characters that no doubt intrigued the average teenager, the films' musical scores were composed of jazz music, not rock 'n' roll.

It was *Blackboard Jungle*, a startling film about a New York City high school plagued by a gang of violent teens, that first proclaimed its provoking message through the adoption of a rock 'n' roll theme song. Based on the best-selling novel *The Blackboard Jungle*, by Evan Hunter, the film opens to the exuberant strains of Haley's recording of "Rock Around the Clock," which sets the tone for the disturbing drama to follow. In his history of rock 'n' roll music, *Flowers in the Dustbin*, James Miller opines that the movie *Blackboard Jungle* "popularized the idea that rock 'n' roll music was about disorder, aggression, and sex: a fantasy of human nature, running wild to a savage beat." When the film debuted, throughout the country the media reported instances of street violence erupting spontaneously outside the theatres after showings.

In one of the movie's most terrifying scenes, a dedicated school-teacher's collection of jazz records is fiercely destroyed by a group of his rock 'n' roll-preferring juvenile-delinquent students. While under-lining the relationship between rock 'n' roll music and misconduct, this scene also underscores one of rock 'n' roll's most remarkable characteristics: the astonishing speed with which the new musical genre exploded. It was during a period of just three years, between 1954 and 1957, that rock 'n' roll emerged, developed, took over teen tastes, and set the trends that forever altered the course of popular music in America. In the 1954 novel upon which *Blackboard Jungle* was based, the juvenile delinquents who destroy the teacher's record collection and criticize his old-fashioned musical tastes taunt him for his ad-miration of musicians who can't stand up to the likes of the singers they revere, such as Perry Como and Tony Bennett. So quickly had rock 'n' roll become *the* youth music of the day that by the time the film came out, just one year after the book, the idea of teens admir-ing pop music performers like Como and Bennett was ludicrously out of date.

Because of its inclusion in *Blackboard Jungle*, "Rock Around the Clock" became a mega-hit recording. Until recently, there had been conflict-ing stories of how the record came to be selected as the film's theme song. But diligent research by Peter Ford has shown the previous stories to be false and the commonly accepted tale of the marriage of "Rock Around the Clock" and *Blackboard Jungle* is now that put forth by Ford.[17] Ford is the son of Hollywood dance star Eleanor Powell and actor Glenn Ford, who played the starring role of the schoolteacher in *Blackboard Jungle*. In the fall of 1954, when Peter Ford was a fifth-grader, and a big fan of rhythm and blues, he acquired a copy of Bill Haley & His Comets' recording of "Rock Around the Clock." Richard Brooks, who directed and wrote the screenplay for *Blackboard Jungle*, heard the recording one day when he was visiting the family home to discuss work on the film with Glenn Ford. Brooks subsequently borrowed Peter Ford's "Rock Around the Clock" record and, upon consulta-tion with assistant director Joel Freeman, decided to use it as the movie's theme song.

MGM, the film studio that was producing *Blackboard Jungle*, pur-chased the rights to use Haley's recording of "Rock Around the Clock" for $5,000 from Decca Records. While the $5,000 bought them permis-sion to use the recording three times within the film, for only $2,500 more the studio could have purchased complete ownership of the song. According to the *Guinness Book of World Records*, "Rock Around the Clock" went on to sell no fewer than 25 million copies. In their effort to save a measly $2,500, MGM missed out on the virtually incalculable amount of money generated by what has come to be considered the seminal rock 'n' roll song.

In linking rock 'n' roll to teen violence, Hollywood gave ammunition to those who objected to rock 'n' roll for other reasons, most notably its deep roots in black culture. It was just 10 months before the release of *Blackboard Jungle* that the Supreme Court handed down its decision in the landmark school desegregation case *Brown v. Board of Education*. Ruling in favor of the African-American plaintiff Oliver Brown, whose daughter had been forced by their local school board to travel to a segregated school far away from her home, the court decreed that the maintenance of racially segregated schools was unconstitutional and would no longer be legally permitted. The decision induced outrage among many parents, whose anger at the prospect of racial integration may have manifested in a lashing out against rock 'n' roll music. Their objections to integration in the classroom could easily have intertwined with disapproval of their youngsters' identification with a heavily black-influenced music that was now also being affiliated with juvenile delinquency. And from there it was a short leap to fears of sexual immorality, as rock 'n' roll's driving beat was said by some to appeal to man's baser instincts.

Initially, Hollywood's association of rock 'n' roll with teenage violence served to promote the music's popularity. The more their parents objected to it, the more the teens liked it. However, it soon became apparent that the sorts of aggressively rebellious and truly deviant teen characters portrayed in such movies as *The Wild One* and *Blackboard Jungle* did not represent the majority of American teenagers. The music industry quickly realized that in order to continue profiting from the teenage rock 'n' roll craze, it would need to soften the music's image in such a way that parents, while they may never like the music, would at least tolerate it. In an effort to capitalize on the trend, Hollywood strategically turned to the production of a new tamer genre of rock 'n' roll films. The sympathetic teenage characters in these films were generally clean-cut and well behaved, yet they harbored a love for rock 'n' roll music, which by the end of the movie they had managed to convince their parents wasn't such a bad thing after all. While these rock 'n' roll films are generally of little cinematic significance, they possess important historical value in that they often include footage of the most influential rock 'n' roll artists of the era performing their biggest hits.

Hurrying to benefit from the success of *Blackboard Jungle,* B-movie specialist Sam Katzman set out to produce a film that would not only feature the sound of rock 'n' roll music, but would go one step further, and show the rock 'n' roll performers in action. It may seem as though Katzman's idea had already been enacted with the October 1955 release of the low-budget film *Rock 'n' Roll Revue.* The name of that film, however, was clearly an attempt to exploit rock 'n' roll's nascent popularity, as the film itself was made up of nothing more than 26 filmed stage performances by the stalwart rhythm and blues artists of the day. (The movie was actually a re-combined re-release of two earlier films: *Rock and Roll Revue,* released on a limited basis in April 1955 and then nationally in August, and *Harlem Variety Revue,* released in May 1955.) Its performers could not really be considered rock 'n' roll musicians. Hosted by Harlem disc jockey Willie Bryant, the movie comprised performances that had been filmed during the summer of 1954 at Harlem's Apollo Theatre with the intention of marketing them as a television series titled "Apollo Varieties." At that time, however, television was uninterested in rhythm and blues programming.[18]

Katzman's film, on the other hand, features performers who could legitimately be categorized as rock 'n' roll artists, most notably Bill Haley & His Comets, who performed their hit "Rock Around the Clock," which became the film's title. The movie also includes performances by two important genre-defining, early rock 'n' roll vocal groups: the Platters, singing their hits "Only You" and "The Great Pretender," and Freddie Bell and the Bellboys, performing "Giddy Up A Ding Dong," which was not a big hit in the United States, but proved popular abroad.

Released in 1956, like *Blackboard Jungle,* the film was criticized for inducing youth violence. Following a showing of *Rock Around the Clock* in Minneapolis, it was reported that a group of teens snake-danced around the town, smashing windows, leading to the cancellation of future screenings of the film at that theatre. Rioting ensued in the wake of overseas showings of *Rock Around the Clock.* The shah of Iran banned the film, deeming it a threat to Iranian civilization.[19]

A box office success, *Rock Around the Clock* became the prototype for Fifties rock 'n' roll films. It showcased popular artists performing their hit songs in musical segments that were not integrated into the plot. The film's storyline included no speaking roles for the musical artists and served mainly to demonstrate adults growing to approve of rock 'n' roll music.

The dancing in *Rock Around the Clock* was largely of the Jitterbug variety (see chapter 2) and occurred during the musical sequences, as teenage characters spontaneously got up and danced to the rock 'n' roll music. While the dancers in the film were supposed to be portraying '50s teens, one must be careful not to assume that the kind of dancing they did was truly representative of the social dancing practiced by average teenagers of the era. As is almost always the case when social dance forms are depicted in stage or screen productions, the dancing is transformed into a theatricalized presentation, the movements designed by a professional choreographer, in this case Earl Barton, and the steps performed by highly trained dancers. While it is accurate to presume that typical teenagers danced the Jitterbug to songs such as "Rock Around the Clock" in social contexts, it is unlikely that they executed the extensive acrobatic maneuvers and the speedy, polished footwork seen in the on-screen choreography. Although daring aerial tricks and fast-moving feet were features of the Lindy Hop, the dance upon which the Jitterbug is based, most teenagers getting up and dancing socially in the '50s would not have had the required skills, rehearsal time, or even dance-floor space needed to perform the kinds of rapid steps, overhead flips, and upside-down lifts featured in the film.

The dancers who performed in the early rock 'n' roll films of the 1950s were the same highly skilled Lindy dancers who had worked in Hollywood movies during the 1940s, performing the Swing dance styles of that era. In numerous personal interviews, conducted by Swing-dance expert Tami Stevens, those Hollywood dancers claimed that when they appeared in '50s rock 'n' roll movies they performed the same Lindy style they had always danced.[20]

In addition to the carry-over of elements from earlier Swing styles, the dancing in *Rock Around the Clock* (and most of the other rock 'n' roll films to follow) exhibited characteristics of theatrical jazz dance and even some classical ballet technique that would not have been in the ordinary movement vocabulary of social-dancing teenagers. Here and there throughout the dance sequences in these films one detects the influence of choreographer Jack Cole. Commonly called "the father of jazz dance," Cole's uniquely fused, Asian- and African-influenced, "cool" dance style exerted tremendous influence on Broadway and Hollywood choreography of the mid-20th century.

Also, the beatnik feel to the costuming and the lingo spouted by the dancers in *Rock Around the Clock*—few of whom look young enough to be playing teenagers—undermines any attempt to realistically reflect the dancing of teenaged rock 'n' roll fans of the '50s. The dance scenes feel like "performances" inspired by more mature sensibilities. An influential American literary and social movement that indeed flourished in the 1950s, the Beat culture was led by bohemian writers and artists who had come of age in the late '40s, and were notably older than the teenagers who embraced early rock 'n' roll. The Beat Generation idolized those who were different or lived outside conventional social systems. They were fascinated with urban black culture, from which they appropriated vocabulary, such as "dig," "cool," "man," and "split."[21] Essentially a fringe movement during the 1950s, it wasn't until its ideas of alternative lifestyles were embraced by the counter-culture youth movement of the 1960s that a Beat influence on rock 'n' roll music could be clearly identified. Harboring more cerebral tastes than the young teens of the 1950s, the Beat Generation preferred listening and contemplating to the progressive sound of bebop jazz than jumping up and down to the repetitive rhythms of rock 'n' roll.

Trying to build on the success of *Rock Around the Clock*, Katzman produced a sequel, *Don't Knock the Rock*, which was released in December 1956. Less remarkable musically than *Rock Around the Clock*, the film's value lies in its inclusion of footage of the early rock 'n' roll star Little Richard (Richard Wayne Penniman) performing "Tutti Frutti" and "Long Tall Sally," two of his biggest hits. The film's dancing has much in common with that of *Rock Around the Clock*. Again choreographed by Barton, it was performed by professionals, who improvised much of their own Swing dancing and aerial tricks.[22] However, in *Don't Knock the Rock*, when Little Richard sings "Tutti Frutti," amateur dance champions Jovada and Jimmy Ballard take the dance floor alone and perform a Jitterbug routine. A brother and sister team, the Ballards were the Rock 'n' Roll division winners at the 1956 Harvest Moon Ball, which was then New York City's premier couples dance contest. While the Rock 'n' Roll division had been called the Lindy Hop since the contest's formal beginning in 1935, the division's name was changed in 1942 to the Jitterbug-Jive, and then, in 1956, to Rock 'n' Roll. Also in 1956, the division rules were changed so that aerial moves were no longer allowed. As the Ballard's Jitterbugging style did not feature aerial work, and because of their background as social dancers, their performance is probably more accurately reflective of the era's social dancing than is the rest of the film's choreography.

Two more low-budget rock 'n' roll films were released in 1956, both of which are noteworthy only because of the musical performances they contain. *Rock, Rock, Rock* features performances by the pioneering rock 'n' roll singer-guitarist Chuck Berry and the seminal rock 'n' roll doo-wop groups Frankie Lymon and the Teenagers, the Moonglows, and the Flamingos. *Shake, Rattle and Rock* features the groundbreaking rock 'n' roll singer-pianist Fats Domino performing his hit "Ain't That a Shame."

Also in 1956 came the release of the first big-budget rock 'n' roll film, *The Girl Can't Help It*. Made in color and starring the iconic 1950s Hollywood sex symbol Jayne Mansfield, *The Girl Can't Help It* is a cut above the other rock 'n' roll genre films. Driven by a strong storyline and sprinkled with witty comedy, it features appearances by the Platters and Fats Domino, as well as an unusually tame performance by Little Richard.

A parody of movie musicals, gangster films, and what it portrays as the mindlessness of the rock 'n' roll craze, *The Girl Can't Help It* lists no choreographer among its creative team. It begins, however, with a choreographic sequence of Jitterbugging couples dancing behind the opening credits. The couples dance with a much bouncier style than the smooth Jitterbuggers in the other films, more accurately reflecting the influence that rock 'n' roll music had on the way the Jitterbug was danced. The aerial element of the dance is reduced to a few short, bumpy tricks, rather than the lengthy, fluidly woven together phrases of difficult lifts and acrobatics showcased by the professionals in *Rock Around the Clock* and its sequel. The steps in this dance sequence are very basic, slower, and less rhythmically complex, more like the footwork real teens would probably have done. But despite the choreography's closer reflection of actual social dancing of the era, the slapstick maneuvers and sense of vaudevillian comedy imbued in the movements display a precision and timing suggestive of rehearsed performances by professional dancers.

Later in the film, however, there is a nightclub scene in which teens (cast age appropriately) dance to Fats Domino's performance of "Blue Monday." Though moving with wild abandon, they do nothing more complicated than a slow Jitterbug basic, some swivel steps, and underarm turns that almost any teenager could execute. Dancing in bare feet, socks, or flat shoes on a crowded dance floor, and performing no showy acrobatics, they can be seen to represent a relatively true picture of the social rock 'n' roll dancing of the times.

Released in 1957, the film *Mr. Rock and Roll* is a loose account of the DJ Alan Freed's role in the transformation of rhythm and blues into rock 'n' roll and the fourth movie in which Freed appeared. (He had been in *Rock Around the Clock, Don't Knock the Rock,* and *Rock, Rock, Rock,* playing himself in each instance.) The movie includes performances by Chuck Berry, Little Richard, and Frankie Lymon and the Teenagers.

Jamboree is another 1957 film that included notable rock 'n' roll performances. A movie about two aspiring singers manipulated by their managers, it features appearances by Fats Domino, the fiery piano-playing rock 'n' roll star Jerry Lee Lewis, and the young teen idol Frankie Avalon. It is hard to categorize the movie, however, as a typical rock 'n' roll genre film, as its musical aesthetic is more eclectic. The film's inclusive lineup of performers represents pop, country, and jazz sounds, as well as rock 'n' roll, and features country singer Slim Whitman as well as the great swing bandleader Count Basie. The group dance numbers in *Jamboree,* which are done as "performances," in a show-within-the-show-style, were choreographed by Broadway's Danny Daniels. The movements, though seasoned with Jitterbug flavorings, are decidedly theatrical in nature and are clearly influenced more by the choreographic style of Broadway dance-maker Bob Fosse than by teenage social dancing of the period.

In 1958, Freed appeared, again as himself, in the film *Go, Johnny, Go!* The film also includes the rare appearance of a rock 'n' roll star, Chuck Berry, in an acting role, albeit portraying a fictionalized version of himself. Despite some entertaining, and slickly choreographed musical sequences, typical of its genre the film is otherwise insignificant. Throughout the 1950s, many more movies were made in exploitation of the rock 'n' roll explosion, most of which were so cheaply and amateurishly produced as to be cinematically embarrassing.

Gyrations of the Rock 'n' Roll Giants

From the outset, rock 'n' roll music was dance music. It arrived at a time when the practice of social dancing was waning, in that the popular music of the day, jazz, was evolving from the dance-inspiring big band, swing music into the more listening-oriented, rhythmically complicated bebop sounds, which could be extremely difficult for an average person to dance to.

Rock 'n' roll music, on the other hand, demanded to be danced to. Perhaps the most convincing evidence of rock 'n' roll's intrinsic power to move people is rooted in what can be considered the "original" rock 'n' roll dances: those spontaneous, improvised, often outrageous movements made by the performers themselves. Not only was it virtually impossible to sit still while listening to rock 'n' roll music, but it also appeared to be impossible to play and sing rock 'n' roll without engaging in some form of inventive "dancing." None of the early rock 'n' roll performers simply stood still and sang. They all moved, usually with furious abandon and often quite provocatively. And the most famously provoking moves were those exhibited by rock 'n' roll's biggest star: Elvis Presley.

Elvis Presley

A superstar of the highest magnitude, Elvis Presley popularized rock 'n' roll on a wider scale than any other single performer. By 1956, he had emerged as the singing sensation of the nation. The esteemed American composer and conductor Leonard Bernstein called Presley "the greatest cultural force in the 20th century."[23]

Growing up in a poor southern family, Presley was exposed as a youngster to both country and western music and to the black musical traditions that fed rhythm and blues. Because of the strong country music sensibility that Presley brought to his singing, he was responsible for pioneering the popular sub-genre of rock 'n' roll that came to be called "rockabilly." In addition to "white" country influences, Presley also brought to rock 'n' roll an exquisite vocal quality—a rich, velvety sound and a wide pitch range—of the sort prized by the pop music world. Epitomizing the hybrid nature of rock 'n' roll music, Presley is probably the performer most responsible for distinguishing rock 'n' roll as its own musical form, separate from the rhythm and blues that constituted so much of its original makeup. Presley was the leader in allowing white America, or those who felt disinclined to embrace "black" music, to claim rock 'n' roll as their own.[24]

Presley's music represented "the coming together of black and white culture into the mainstream in a way that had never happened before," wrote the Pulitzer Prize–winning journalist David Halberstam in *The*

Elvis Presley, the seminal rock 'n' roll superstar, performing for ecstatic fans in the 1950s. While arousing to teens, Presley's physical gyrations shocked older audiences. (Photo by Michael Ochs Archives/Getty Images)

Fifties, his analytical account of the decade's cultural trends. When Presley was interviewed on the air following the first radio play of his music, the disc jockey asked Presley what high school he had attended. As the show was being broadcast in the then-segregated South, the question was the DJ's strategic way of indicating to his listeners that, though he may have evoked decidedly black musical qualities, the singer they had just heard was white. The Memphis-based record producer Sam Phillips, the man who discovered Presley's talents, is often credited with "inventing" Presley, as it was Phillips who encouraged the singer's melding of country and rhythm and blues. Phillips said that he always knew "if I could find a white boy who could sing like a black man I'd make a million dollars."[25]

With his seductive good looks, sexy smile, and arresting black hair, Presley was catnip for adolescent girls, yet created an uproar among the older generation, who viewed him as a threat to their conservative sensibilities. Presley's shock appeal, however, probably resulted more from his physical movements than from his singing. When Presley sang, particularly up-tempo songs, it was as if the music was percolating inside his body and completely overtaking him physically. There was a seamless connection between his body movements, the musical accompaniment, and the vocal sounds he was producing.

While he sang this new "integrated" music, he exuded a steamy sensuality that was underlined by his dance-like actions. Strong, sudden bursts of movement would charge out of his body, as if emanating from a whirling current of electricity stored up deep within his torso. He kept the beat of the music by bouncing on his heels or by accentuating the beat with knee pops—a quick release and percussive straightening of the knee joints. One of his signature moves was a punctuating action in which he made two quick movements of one bent knee—across and open. A sharp and explicit opening of his thighs, the move, whether Presley intended it or not, was undeniably sexual.

When he sang, Presley's head sat loosely on his neck. He rarely looked skyward, more often than not tilting his chin downward in a way that allowed him to focus alluringly on individual female audience members. His head moved around as if impelled by a low heat simmering somewhere deep within his throat. When he was not accompanying himself on the guitar, his arms hung freely at his sides and would dart out periodically to gesture to the audience. His arm movements varied widely, but always seemed to be authentic responses to the song lyrics or the musical dynamics. When Presley sang slow, quiet songs, strumming his guitar, he emanated a softer energy, but his characteristic sudden ticks of movement still came out on accented notes. He would shimmy his shoulders or do single-shoulder lifts or rolls that were so small and unexpected that they felt to viewers like secret sexy surprises.

Because his physicality was such an integral part of his performance persona, when the new medium of television finally began to take an interest in rock 'n' roll performers, it magnified Presley's impact. The singer was first seen on television on January 28, 1956, on *Stage Show*, a music variety program hosted by the swing-era musicians Tommy and Jimmy Dorsey, and produced by the comedian Jackie Gleason. When Merrill Staton was invited to perform as a back-up singer for Presley on *Stage Show*, he agreed, but opted to sing off-stage. A highly regarded professional singer, with a doctorate in Music Education from Columbia University's Teachers College, Staton was reluctant to be seen with the gyrating guitarist. And when Presley instructed Staton on how he wanted him to sing, Staton said, "OK, but I can't do those moves."[26]

Presley was introduced to the *Stage Show* viewers as a young hillbilly singer, and re-appeared on the program in February and March. His performances were said to include lots of pelvic gyrations, which garnered him the nickname "Elvis the Pelvis." Members of the show's largely middle-aged audience were generally revolted by Presley's performances, and responded with the sending of much unfavorable mail.[27]

On April 3, 1956, Presley appeared on the television variety show hosted by the comedian Milton Berle. The show's viewers were polarized in their response to Presley. While younger viewers went absolutely wild over the new rock 'n' roll idol, the reaction from older viewers may have been more in line with that of television critic Jack Gould who, writing in the *New York Times* on June 6, 1956, described Presley as "a rock 'n' roll variation of one of the most standard acts in show business: the virtuoso of the hootchy-kootchy." Reviewing Presley's performance in the *New York Journal-American*, Jack O'Brien called the singer's movements "plainly planned, suggestive animation short of an aborigine's mating dance."[28]

Most of the outrage caused by Presley's "dancing" seems sparked by what were commonly referred to as his pelvis movements. On occasion, Presley would accentuate a musical beat or phrase ending with an erotic jolting action, a strong, forward pelvic thrust, like a stripper's bump. Close observation, however, reveals that while many of his other actions did indeed involve surges of movement through his lower body, he did not generally move his pelvis in an isolated fashion, as would a jazz dancer, or the striptease artist trying to suggest sexually oriented maneuvers. Presley's lower-body movements, though unquestionably sexy in effect, do not appear initiated by contractions or relaxations of the core muscles of the pelvic and abdominal regions, but seem to be generated largely by his legs and thighs. He often rotated his legs inward and outward as he skid sensually along the floor or posed in mid-level lunges, in which he then alternated the bend in his knee from one leg to the other, or opened one thigh with a seductive circling action. His moves did not evoke a sleazy feel, as much as a snazzy, stylish quality.

But so fierce were adult objections to Presley that it was only after the singer's performance on the variety show hosted by Steve Allen that the famous Sunday night variety show host Ed Sullivan re-considered his previously firm refusal to allow Presley to appear on his family-oriented program. On July 1, 1956, the night Presley appeared on Allen's show, which was broadcast on Sundays opposite Sullivan's, the ratings for Sullivan's program nose-dived.

It seems apparent that the excited reactions to Presley's television appearances had as much, if not more, to do with his movements than with his singing. It has been widely publicized that Sullivan vehemently insisted that when Presley sang on his show he was to be filmed only from the waist up, so that audiences would not be exposed to any potentially offensive pelvic motions. In reality, however, Presley's full body was in the shot during much of his singing on Sullivan's program. Presley made three appearances on *The Ed Sullivan Show* (on September 9 and October 28, 1956, and on January 6, 1957), singing a combination of ballads and up-tempo numbers. It was only during the 1957 broadcast that the lower half of Presley's body was kept out of camera range. But regardless of the degree of control Sullivan ultimately did or did not exert on how Presley was filmed, it cannot be denied that the legendary status of the story, and the public's overwhelming concern with it, reveal much about the era's attitudes toward sex and expressive physical movements. It also underlines the intrinsic connections between body movement and the emergence of rock 'n' roll.

Quick to latch on to the Presley phenomenon, beginning with *Love Me Tender* in November 1956, Hollywood produced six movies in the 1950s (and 25 more in the Sixties) featuring Presley. The other five were *Loving You* (July 1957), *Jailhouse Rock* (November 1957), *King Creole* (July 1958), *G.I. Blues* (November 1960), and *Flaming Star* (December 1960). But unlike the typical rock 'n' roll genre films, in which the musical artists simply made appearances performing their songs in musical segments unrelated to the plot, Presley's films featured him in leading acting and singing roles. While the movies were tailor-made vehicles for Presley and fared well at the box office, they were not highly regarded by film critics.

Chuck Berry, Little Richard, Jerry Lee Lewis, and Fats Domino

Aside from Presley, in the inaugural phase of rock 'n' roll music, the most important solo trailblazers were Chuck Berry, Little Richard, Jerry Lee Lewis, and Fats Domino. With the unprecedented speed at which rock 'n' roll developed, the popularity of individual songs often rose and fell with extraordinary rapidity. Two months was the longevity average of hit records in the 1950s.[29] And the fame of the artists who recorded them came and went with a similar velocity. The history of rock 'n' roll is peopled by many performers, who had one or two big hits, and were never heard of again. Berry, Little Richard, Lewis, and Domino stand out, however, as not only were they responsible for the birth of rock 'n' roll, but they managed to sustain their popularity for many years. Like Presley, each one exhibited dynamic, highly individualized movement styles. The "dancing" they did as they sang and played their instruments was inseparable from their music-making and became an integral part of their celebrity personas.

Rock 'n' roll trailblazer Chuck Berry doing his famous "duck walk." (Library of Congress)

In delineating the history of rock 'n' roll music in his book *The Sound of the City: The Rise of Rock and Roll*, British musicologist Charlie Gillett wrote, "If importance in popular music were measured in terms of imaginativeness, creativeness, wit, the ability to translate a variety of experiences and feelings into musical form, and long-term influence and reputation, Chuck Berry would be described as the major figure of rock 'n' roll." Berry was also the inventor of a signature movement, his "duck walk," which may be considered the very first rock 'n' roll dance step. While playing his guitar, holding it down against his hip and off to one side, Berry would bend his knees into a low, almost squatting position. In this earthy, rounded posture, he would proceed across the stage, lifting his knees, flexing his ankles, and sometimes jutting his chin quickly and sharply forward in double-time to his steps. When he reached the end of the stage space, he would turn abruptly and proceed back in the other direction. Berry also developed a signature one-legged hopping movement that he did while playing his guitar. Both moves have become emblematic of Berry and the theatrical nature of his animated performing style.

An explosive singer, Little Richard contributed enormously to defining not only the sound but also the untamed character of early rock 'n' roll. Sporting a six-inch-high pompadour, with his bizarre mannerisms, excessive energy, and over-the-top showmanship, Little Richard put on a wild stage act that defied any sense of decorum or predictability. When accompanying himself on the piano, he generally stood up and bounced to the beat with his knees. He might turn around and play the keyboard with his arms behind his back, rocking side to side. Sometimes he lifted his leg and placed it atop the piano, continuing to strike the keys with one arm on either side of his thigh, as he lifted the hip of his raised leg up and down in time to the music. The effect was one of raw eroticism. In his singing, he accented important lyrics or phrase endings with huge dramatic moves. For instance, at climactic points in "Long Tall Sally" in the film *Don't Knock the Rock*, he can be seen making a big backward circle with his arms before leaning back and plunging into an off-kilter lunge position. Little Richard was later known to leap up on top of the piano and jump down from it, or hurl himself off the stage and run frenetically up and down the aisles of the theatre. His goal was to incite a sense of total freedom and frenzy. The unexpectedness of his movements and the large amounts of space they engulfed made a strong visual and kinesthetic contribution to his ability to startle

Flamboyant rock 'n' roll star Little Richard performing one of his audacious sig-nature moves on a Hollywood film set in the late 1950s. (Photo by Frank Driggs Collection/Getty Images)

audiences and shake up their thinking about conventional notions of socially acceptable behavior.

Another wild man on the rock 'n' roll stage, Jerry Lee Lewis sang while playing the piano in a violent hammering style. He was known for his technique of manipulating the emotional pitch of his music by building to intense peaks and then slackening off, only to build up again to another climax.[30] A truly ferocious man at the piano, Lewis sat on the bench with his legs spread apart, his body angled slightly out to the audience, and his front leg opening in and out as his thigh traveled back and forth across the bench. He kept the beat with his feet, his toes pumping up and down, creating a crazed impression. Sometimes he would kick the piano bench out from underneath himself and keep pounding away at the keys while standing in a deep knee bend hunched over the instrument. His most famous hits were the songs "Great Balls of Fire" and "Whole Lotta Shakin' Goin' On."

Pioneering rock 'n' roll pianist-singer Jerry Lee Lewis, known for his wild antics at the keyboard. (Warner Bros./Photofest)

A singer-pianist in the jump blues style, Fats Domino was perhaps the most universally appealing of this first crop of rock 'n' roll stars. Though lively and very danceable, his music was less assaultive than that of the others. He planted his bulky frame firmly on the piano bench as he played and sang, but constantly shifted his weight around in easy curving pathways. Sometimes he'd make a big circle with his torso, or round forward over the piano, and then lean way back, or twist to open himself to the audience. There was a very relaxed quality to how he held his torso, a looseness in the middle that allowed his rib cage to sometimes shift independently in either direction or to curve forward. His head would tip, sometimes sideways, sometimes forward, and his shoulders might lift and pulse downward to the beat. Like his music, his brand of movement evoked a disarming, easy, and comfortable quality.

The Platters, a doo-wop group, seen here in the mid-1950s. The synchronized, gestural choreography of Fifties vocal groups was reflected in the social group dances invented by the era's teens. (Photofest)

Vocal Groups

The popular early rock 'n' roll vocal groups also exhibited distinctive movement traits. Mirroring the tightness of their harmonies, they tended to move in tightly synchronized unison. Unlike the soloists, these singers performed choreographed actions that were clearly rehearsed, rather than seemingly spontaneous. The choreography would include small step-touch patterns, sways, turns, pivots, tiny kicks or knee lifts, and an assortment of hand gestures that gave them a highly stylized look and feel. This kind of choreography was further developed by the soul singers who flourished in the 1960s and evolved into one of the signature elements of the Motown era.

While their movements played significant roles in the generating and popularizing of their music, none of these groundbreaking rock 'n' roll artists could be considered a truly gifted dancer. (The first influential rock 'n' roll musician who could claim that honor would be soul singer James Brown.) However, the two differing kinds of body movements put forth by the original rock 'n' roll stars—the highly animated, impulsive gyrations of the solo singers and the smooth, slick moves of the doo-woppers—can be seen to parallel the two major categories of rock 'n' roll dancing that were to develop among teenagers in the 1950s. To the spirited fast songs, teens generally improvised freely and wildly, albeit within the Jitterbug form. But to the calmer songs, they wound up creating group-oriented dances built of prescribed moves, performed in specific formations, and often mirroring a song's lyrics.

So what exactly happened when the Fifties teens got out of their seats and began dancing to this infectious, revolutionary music? What did they do with their bodies? What did their dancing represent? And what kind of reverberations resulted from their dancing to rock 'n' roll music?

2

The Rock 'n' Roll
Dance Floor

It was the natural combustion of teenage physicality and the youth culture's tumultuous new music that spawned the social rock 'n' roll dancing of the 1950s. Yet from a purely terpsichorean viewpoint, the dancing was not particularly original. When the teens danced to fast rock 'n' roll songs, they generally did the Jitterbug, a dance that had been around since the 1930s. And while the teens did invent some new dances, there was nothing terribly remarkable about the actual dance steps nor the artistry, choreographic aesthetics, technical characteristics, athleticism, or visual design of most of what they created. It was the dancers themselves, the music, and the time period that lends cultural significance to what occurred on the rock 'n' roll dance floors of the 1950s. A spanking new social demographic emblematically moved their bodies to ferociously fresh music in an era when multitudinous American traditions were also being fiercely shaken up.

The rock 'n' roll music of the 1950s was extremely easy to dance to because it had a steady, straightforward beat. And the extraordinarily uninhibited nature of the music prompted even the most insecure or self-conscious listener to feel he could join in the action. When the film *Blackboard Jungle* opened in Boston, teenagers jumped up out of their seats and began dancing in the aisles as soon as they heard the movie's rousing rock 'n' roll theme song, "Rock Around the Clock." Unable to stop the teens from dancing, the theater management proceeded to show the opening of the film with the sound turned down, so the music couldn't be heard.[1]

Betty Romantini was a teenager in the 1950s in Philadelphia where she danced on the famous television program *American Bandstand* (see chapter 3). She recalled how she felt when listening to WDAS, a black-oriented radio station that played the rhythm and blues music that morphed into early rock 'n' roll: "You just wanted to get up and dance . . . you felt it in your soul. It was the kind of music . . . you internalized and your body just went with it. And teenagers all over were having the same kind of experience. . . . Our parents, the older generation didn't get it and I think it frightened them. It appeared to them that we were out of control."[2]

Rock 'n' Roll Riots

Many '50s teens were inspired to dance by the music they heard on the radio. But the beginnings of rock 'n' roll social dancing as a mass phenomenon can be traced to the enormous concert events at which teenage audiences heard, watched, and were impelled to move by the often raucous performances of the early rock 'n' roll musical artists.

Deejay Alan Freed, who had become well known as a producer of live music and dance events, presented a "Rock 'n' Roll Easter Jubilee" at Brooklyn's Paramount Theatre, on April 12, 1955. A proscenium theater space, the venue did not lend itself to dancing by audience members. Nonetheless, incapable of sitting still while listening to Freed's electrifying line-up of rock 'n' roll artists, the teenage audience danced wildly out into the aisles and atop their seats. They jumped up and down with such force that many of the theater seats had to be repaired following the concert.[3]

In 1956, in response to the dancing that large groups of teenagers were doing to rock 'n' roll music, the Los Angeles County Board of Supervisors re-instated a Progressive Era law prohibiting public dancing in parks and open spaces. It was claimed that such dancing might contribute to increased juvenile delinquency. All public dances were henceforth required to obtain prior approval by the Board of Education and, in effect, had to be held on school grounds, where rock 'n' roll music and interracial dancing could be banned. In Atlanta, a similar law was enacted, barring teens from dancing in public without the written consent of their parents.[4]

While the screening of films containing rock 'n' roll music and the presentation of live concerts proved stirring enough individually, it

Rowdy teens moving to the rock 'n' roll music at a 1957 concert. (© Bettmann/ Corbis)

was not unusual for big rock 'n' roll events in the 1950s to incorporate both a movie showing and onstage performances in a single event—following the long-standing movie-theater tradition of films and a live show. Some teens remember attending concerts at a drive-in movie theater where, in between film screenings, the rock 'n' roll acts performed atop the roof of the little building that served as the venue's refreshment stand.[5]

In 1957 a two-day, combined rock 'n' roll concert and movie-screening event, produced by Freed at Manhattan's Paramount Theater, featured showings of the new film *Don't Knock the Rock* and performances by 12 different top rock 'n' roll artists. By the time the venue opened at 8:15 A.M., 5,000 teenagers were already in line for admission to the 3,650-seat theater, and throughout the day a continuous stream of more than 15,000 teens queued up to see the shows.[6] According to the *New York Times*, the crowd inside the theater danced in the aisles, the foyer, and the lobby and stood in their seats, jumped up and down, and stamped their feet in time with the music. The rambunctious foot stomping prompted the worried theater owners to call

Hordes of teens trying to get into a combined rock 'n' roll concert and film-showing event at the Paramount Theater in New York City. (Photo by Frank Driggs Collection/Getty Images)

in the Fire Department, and it was decided to take the precautionary measure of removing 1,000 of the teenagers from the protruding balcony sections.[7] The next day, when more than 16,000 teens showed up, 279 New York City police officers and 25 theater police were assigned to the theater. They patrolled the aisles, chasing would-be dancers back to their seats and ordering those who stood in their seats to sit down.[8]

Freed's 1958 "Big Beat Rock 'n' Roll Show" at the Boston Arena drew 6,000 fans and turned into a wild melee when the police would not allow the house lights to be turned off during the concert. It was reported that in the ensuing fight between the teens and the police 15 people were slugged, beaten, or robbed by a berserk gang of teenagers.[9]

These live rock 'n' roll music and dance events routinely attracted large, highly spirited crowds. If contemporary newspaper reporting is to be believed, the concerts regularly evoked riotous behavior, which did much to feed the anti–rock 'n' roll feelings among the general populace. It is impossible to determine, however, whether the reported violence was always initiated by the teens. It may have been instigated to some degree by overly zealous authorities fearful of what might transpire with such large gatherings of teens under the influence of the invigorating new music.

A disturbance at an early rock 'n' roll concert in New Haven, Connecticut, caused the police from the neighboring town of Bridgeport to institute a ban on rock 'n' roll dances anywhere in their jurisdiction. The ban forced the cancellation of an upcoming concert by Fats Domino who, ironically, was one of the tamest of the early rock 'n' rollers.[10] After some audience members got rowdy at one of Freed's shows in Hartford, Connecticut, controlling authorities decided to cancel many of the DJ's upcoming concerts, including events in Troy, New York, and in Jersey City, New Jersey. At a live rock 'n' roll show in Lewiston, Maine, a 14-year-old boy was arrested for climbing onto the stage and trying to dance.[11] In light of all the commotion in other cities, the Washington, D.C., police chief proposed a ban on rock 'n' roll shows at the National Guard Armory.[12]

While hearing and seeing the provocative rock 'n' roll artists perform incited physical responses from the teens, it was not just the live concerts that evoked disruptive activity. It seems that even hearing the recorded rock 'n' roll music played by DJs at record hops (see below) prompted objectionable behavior. Record hop riots were reported in numerous cities, including Birmingham, Alabama, and Boston and Cambridge, Massachusetts. Rioting in Cleveland spurred city officials to unearth an old ordinance that barred anyone under the age of 18 from dancing in a public place. DJs in that city were required to obtain special police permission if they wanted to hold teen dances.[13]

In 1957, an associate in psychiatry at Columbia University suggested parallels between rock 'n' roll dancing and both the crazed moves of the St. Vitus dancers of the Middle Ages and the manic movements of mad victims of toxic tarantula bites. He described the dancing teens of the 1950s as "moved by a juke box to dance themselves more and more into a prehistoric rhythmic trance until it had gone far beyond all the accepted versions of human dancing."[14] While his trance claims are certainly debatable, his description of the dancing represents how many rock 'n' roll opponents viewed the kinds of physical activity the music was inducing. The media reinforced such opinions, as newspaper and magazines nationwide rarely missed an opportunity to underline the relationship between rock 'n' roll music events and rowdy teen behavior.

Embodying Racial Integration

While it may have been the violence and wild cavorting that captured the headlines, what made the early rock 'n' roll concert and dance events truly groundbreaking was their unusual embodiment of racial integration. Not only did the music reflect a blending of black and white sensibilities, but the audiences were composed of a combination of black and white youth that was unforeseen in America. In many areas of the country during the 1950s, the black and white segments of the population were segregated in all aspects of their lives—their schooling, housing, recreational activities, socializing, church-going, and attendance at arts and entertainment performances. Suddenly, with the white teens' burgeoning interest in rock 'n' roll, which in the early days was essentially the rhythm and blues music that had been popular only in African-American communities, black and white young people were suddenly attending the same concerts. When Freed produced his first live New York City concert and dance event, "The Rock 'n' Roll Jubilee Ball," held on January 14, 1955, the audience was almost exactly half white and half black. It was the first time such a ratio had occurred at a concert of what was primarily rhythm and blues music.[15]

At most of the early rock 'n' roll concert and dance events in the South, where segregation was legally mandated, the audience would be divided by race, with blacks on one side of the venue and whites on the other, or perhaps with one race upstairs and the other downstairs. At other times a rope would separate black and white audience members. Yet while the teens may have started out on their respective sides of the rope, it was not uncommon, as they danced, for the white teens to move up close to the rope, trying to get a better view, as they watched and copied the dance steps the black teenagers were doing. On occasion, the rope would fall down and black and white teens could find themselves dancing together. The anger provoked by such racial intermingling did much to fuel anti-rock 'n' roll sentiments among southern segregationists. Asa Carter, of the Alabama White Citizens Council, described these rock 'n' roll dances as "a plot to mongrelize America."[16]

Even in the North, anti-integration attitudes often prevailed. In 1953, while on a high school junior-class boat trip down the Delaware River in Pennsylvania, two teens starting Jitterbugging together.

"They were the best Jitterbuggers in the class, so the two of them always danced together," recalled the faculty member who was chaperoning the trip. "No one thought anything of it at school functions." The problem, however, was that the girl was white, and the boy was black, and they were dancing together in public. A member of the boat crew quietly went over to the couple and told them they had to stop dancing together, though he said nothing to any of the other, non-interracial teenage couples who were dancing to the musical entertainment on the boat. He then asked them who was in charge of their group. "And he came over and reprimanded me severely for permitting them to dance with one another," said the teacher.[17]

The seeds of racial integration and civil rights were just being planted in the United States during the 1950s. It was in 1955 that the African-American woman Rosa Parks was arrested and jailed for refusing to give up her seat on the bus to a white man. The incident prompted a 382-day boycott by blacks of the city bus system in Montgomery, Alabama. And in 1957, it was necessary to enlist the National Guard to enforce the integration of Little Rock Central High School in Arkansas. The sharing of the rock 'n' roll experience by black and white teenagers during this period represented a bold rejection, by the teens, of the adult culture's longstanding racist attitudes. It also undoubtedly contributed to the progressive racial attitudes the younger generation would adopt and later demonstrate in their support of the Civil Rights Movement of the 1960s and their continued fights against racial prejudice in years to follow.

Sexual Overtones

Like virtually all American vernacular dance styles, the rock 'n' roll dancing of the 1950s was rooted in African-American culture. Repeatedly throughout American history, blacks invented dances that were seen, either informally or through theatrical presentations, by whites who subsequently appropriated them as part of the mainstream popular-dance culture. The Charleston, Lindy, Jitterbug, Tap, and hip-hop—all originated in black communities, were adopted by whites, and are now vital components of the canon of American vernacular dance.

The dancing that evolved in response to rock 'n' roll music is no different from other American vernacular forms, in terms of its

African-American origins. The formidable bond between rock 'n' roll music and movement, the music's commanding ability to make the listener get up and dance, is one strong indicator of its African-influenced roots. In African cultures, dancing is often viewed as a way of heightening the pleasure of listening to music, as it involves oneself in the musical event.[18] "Neither the music, the song, nor the dance stands alone in African-American culture," wrote Benita Junette Brown in a dissertation on African-American grassroots dancing. Also, Brown interprets the improvisational element of American social dancing as a manifestation of the African tradition of needing to make a soulful, personal response to music.[19] Hence, the heavy emphasis on personal improvisation in rock 'n' roll dancing can be viewed as an African characteristic.

While the Jitterbug (see below) has clearly traceable roots in African-American culture, many of the other dances that teenagers created to rock 'n' roll songs during the 1950s were also invented by blacks. Though whites may have popularized them, the dances were often based on steps and body movements the white teens copied from their black peers. In his study of social dance in Philadelphia's African-American community, folklorist John Roberts quotes a black man recalling his teenage years in the 1950s. "In high school," the man said, "during lunch there were always dances; we could always dance in the gym. And many of the white kids would ask us, 'How do you do this? And how do you do that?'" The white kids he was referring to were dancers on *American Bandstand*, the television show that set the teen rock 'n' roll dance trends for the entire country (see chapter 3).[20]

But while, historically, whites have eagerly adopted black dances, they oftentimes felt the need to "clean up" the movements. In white eyes, the social dancing done by blacks was often too overtly sexual. It is likely that this perception derived from the black dancers' extensive use of isolations, which is a technical dance term for isolated movements of a single body part, such as the pelvis, the rib cage, a shoulder, or the head. While independent movements of the arms and legs are a common characteristic of European social, folk, and theatrical dance traditions, in most European-rooted dance forms the torso is held together and moves as a unit. However, as they allow the dancer to simultaneously embody or accent different rhythms of the, often polyrhythmic, African music, isolated movements of distinct parts of the torso are a primary element of many kinds of West African dance.

In that most of the enslaved Africans brought to America came from the western region of the continent, it is West African traditions that form the cultural backgrounds of the majority of African Americans. While in white societies isolated movements of the pelvis might be blatant indications of sexual intent, the same may not be true in an African-American social dance. It is dangerous, therefore, to interpret the meaning of social dance movements that come from one culture through the lens of another. (It is interesting to note that, among Africans, dancing in the European fashion with one arm around your partner's waist was considered obscene, as the African dance culture does not condone bodily contact.)[21]

So was Presley being intentionally "sexual" when he accented phrase endings with his pelvis, or was he just imitating a black movement tradition as he performed songs that were deeply rooted in black musical traditions? And can the rock 'n' roll dancing of the '50s teens, which grew out of African-American music and dancing, genuinely be labeled as sexually subversive? Were the teens really behaving sexually or just rhythmically?

Outside of the South, where racism grounded much of the disapproval of rock 'n' roll, the most violent opposition to the music came from Boston, where the city's Roman Catholic hierarchy branded it "immoral."[22] But it was the perceived lasciviousness of the dancing that rock 'n' roll provoked, more so than the music itself, that really seemed to bother the religious leaders. Anthropologist Cynthia Novack felt that with rock 'n' roll dancing came a permission to move independently and improvisatorially, which became associated with a feeling of spontaneity and with the perception that the dancers were letting go, instead of taking control.[23] Such unbridled physicality—particularly when it involved isolated movements of individual parts of the torso—could certainly be perceived as a threat to the church-supported sexual restraint of the 1950s, as well as a foreshadowing of the Free Love movement of the Sixties.

While influential elements of the adult population objected vehemently to rock 'n' roll in the 1950s, social dance-lovers and those who made their living from social dancing—club owners and dance instructors, for example—offered convincing arguments in support of the new music. Their defense of rock 'n' roll stemmed not from its artistic merit, as most serious musicians agreed it was a terribly simplistic musical form, certainly as compared to jazz, classical music, or many genres of world music. What was so appealing about rock 'n' roll was that it got young people dancing again, as opposed to the largely un-danceable, experimental jazz music of the immediate postwar era, which had significantly squelched participation in social dancing.

Also, dancing to rock 'n' roll was seen as a healthy way for adolescents to blow off the angry steam they harbor during what is typically a conflicted developmental stage. A similar argument was put forth in support of the hip-hop dance forms that emerged in the 1970s. With their highly athletic, competitive qualities they were promoted as positive alternatives to participation in street violence, as they allowed neighborhood gangs to "fight" with one another in the safe context of a "dance floor."

While the large rock 'n' roll concert events afforded teens opportunities to share music and movement experiences with those of different races and backgrounds, the crowded conditions did not support widespread or concentrated dance activity. Most of the more complicated, focused dancing by the teens happened at smaller, local gatherings.

Juke Joints

Many of the commercial establishments frequented by teenagers in the 1950s, such as ice cream parlors, bowling alleys, roller rinks, diners, and drive-in burger joints, provided jukeboxes stocked with the latest rock 'n' roll records. Jukeboxes of that era were coin-operated machines that automatically played 45 rpm records, which listeners selected from a list of song titles. Some of the establishments also had wallboxes, a more compact, tableside device that the teens could use to choose the songs they wanted to hear. Any place that had a jukebox was called a "juke joint," and it was at such locales that teens would commonly gather to dance to the latest rock 'n' roll hits. The mainstream slang term "juke joint" is not to be confused with the, albeit related, African-American vernacular term "jook joint," which refers to black music and dance establishments that emerged just after the Civil War, usually in rural areas of the South. Jook joint derives from the word "jooking," a black slang term that refers to any social form of singing, dancing, or playing, and can carry a somewhat naughty connotation.[24]

Teenagers social dancing at a neighborhood malt shop in the 1950s. It was at such locales, which often had jukeboxes, that Fifties teens would gather to dance to rock 'n' roll music. (© Michael Ochs Archives/Corbis)

Sock Hops

Probably the most influential arena for the development of early rock 'n' roll dancing was the local record hop. While sometimes a live band would provide the music for neighborhood teen rock 'n' roll dance events, more often than not the dances would be hosted by a disc jockey who would play an array of the latest popular records for the teens' listening and dancing pleasure. The dances might be organized by a radio station in conjunction with a sponsor, such as a soda company, or they might be sponsored by a recreational center, church, or school. Originally known as record hops, these events were sometimes held in church basements, fire halls, community centers, old theaters, ballrooms, or roller rinks. Most commonly, however, the dances took place in school gymnasiums. As the school sports coaches generally did not permit the wearing of hard-soled street shoes on the varnished, wooden gym floors, the teens were encouraged to remove their shoes and dance in just their socks. Thus, the dances came to be called "sock hops." The term eventually became a synonym for "record hop" and was widely applied to any 1950s rock 'n' roll dance party, even those held in venues other than gymnasiums, where the removal of shoes was not required.

Neighborhood events, these get-togethers allowed for the invention, observation, and practice of new dance trends, albeit within a decidedly social setting. The famous rock 'n' roll television host Dick Clark (see chapter 3) always felt that teens attended his record hops more for the "mating game" aspect than for the music and dancing.[25] Yet it was at these local community dance events that rock 'n' roll dancing really developed, which is why its earliest forms were highly regionalized. The style of teen dancing could vary distinctively from one part of the country to another, or subtly from neighborhood to neighborhood within the same city. Essentially, however, in the earliest days of rock 'n' roll, it was some version of the Jitterbug that

High school students dancing to rock 'n' roll music in a scene set at a sock hop, from the nostalgic 1973 film *American Graffiti*. Sock hops, typically held in school gymnasiums, were popular arenas for '50s rock 'n' roll dancing. (MCA/Universal Pictures/Photofest)

everyone danced to the fast songs, and a markedly simple form of sensual slow dancing that was done to the ballads.

Jitterbug

The Jitterbug is an offshoot of the Lindy Hop, a high-energy, athletic dance that was started by African Americans at Harlem's Savoy Ballroom in the late 1920s. The dance's risk-taking acrobatic style developed in the 1930s as competing black dancers at the Savoy tried to outdo one another with the invention of ever-more-challenging aerial maneuvers performed with awe-inspiring speed and energy.

A spot dance (it does not travel around the floor), the Lindy is done with a partner, though it employs a looser and lower handhold and a more casual, relaxed body posture than do the standard ballroom dances. The basic step is a syncopated two-step that accentuates the off-beat, followed by a "breakaway," which is the characteristic feature of the dance. It is during the breakaway that the dancers get to show off their tricks and original specialty moves.[26]

Named in 1927, allegedly in honor of Charles Lindbergh's courageous flight across the Atlantic Ocean that year, by the mid-1930s the Lindy was being danced all across the country to the infectious new jazz dance music of the day, which was known as swing. Minus the daring aerial work that was done by the competitors at the Savoy and the professional troupes of Lindy Hoppers who appeared in movies, Broadway musicals, and nightclub shows, the Lindy as danced by the general public emphasized lively, rhythmic foot patterns and fun, brisk partnering that matched the fluid swing sounds of the era's popular big bands.

During the 1930s, the term "jitterbugs" arose as a description of especially raucous swing music fans. In the early 1940s, the term "Jitterbug" started to be used to denote the modified version of the Lindy that Americans nationwide were dancing to the latest swing tunes. (Outside of the United States, the dance was referred to as "Jive.")[27] It is interesting to note that about 70 years after the rise of the Jitterbug, the Samsung electronics company came out with a new cell phone aimed at older-adult markets. The phone was advertised in 2010 as having bigger buttons, bigger numbers, and the capacity to reduce background noise, making the voice sounds easier to hear. Clearly designed for those who had come of age during the Swing era, and might now be having problems seeing and hearing, the phone was cleverly named in such a way as to remind the seniors of a time in their life when they felt young and hip: the name of the phone is the "Jitterbug."[28]

Though movement invention and the freedom to improvise were hallmarks of the Lindy and the Swing dancing that followed, as the Jitterbug exploded in popularity it was soon codified by dance instructors, who profited from teaching a basic form of it at franchised and independent dance studios all across the country. In its codified form the Jitterbug makes use of three versions of a six-count basic step: a single, double, or triple. (The Lindy basic is an eight-count step.) Though it is always in 2/4 or 4/4 meter, the tempo of swing music varies widely. The single basic, therefore, can be used for faster music, as it includes just two slow steps (two counts each), followed by two quick steps done with one leg behind the other and known as a rock-step. The triple basic replaces each of the two slow steps with a triple-step, three steps done to a "one-and-two" rhythm. It is the double version of the basic step, however, that was employed when the Jitterbug was adapted to fit the rock 'n' roll music of the 1950s.[29]

In the double version, each slow step is replaced by a tap-step, which injects a sharp, jerky bounce into the dance, robbing it of the smooth quality it often sported during the Swing era, when the dancing flowed more horizontally and exhibited more rhythmic continuity. Responding to the heavy two-beat pulse of the rock 'n' roll music of the '50s, the Jitterbug became choppier, and was danced with a more upright posture. Also, some dancers replaced the rock step with a kick-ball-change, or eliminated it entirely in favor of two forward walking steps, characteristic of the slotted style of Swing dancing that developed in California and came to be called West Coast Swing in the 1960s. (The East Coast or Savoy style of the Lindy Hop is done in a circular form.)[30]

The real fun of the Jitterbug, however, lies in the vast variety of nifty partner movements that a couple can learn, imitate, or improvise on their own. Jitterbugging can involve fast underarm spins, turning movements that allow the partners to travel together and away from one another or into different side-by-side positions, and constantly changing hand-holds and arm movements, which is generally what the leader uses to guide his partner through all the snazzy moves he wants to make.

A couple slow dancing in the background while others Jitterbug, in a scene from *The Delinquents*, directed by Robert Altman. A 1957 exploitation film about juvenile crime, the movie represents Altman's first feature film and was made in Kansas City, Missouri, the director's hometown. (United Artists/Photofest)

The freedom it gave dancers—to improvise and to impulsively respond to the music through individually styled movements—explains in large part why the Jitterbug remained the dance of choice for young teens wanting to move to fast rock 'n' roll songs. Most teenagers learned the dance from their parents, or from watching friends do it at parties or record hops. The basic patterns of the Jitterbug provided a secure structure within which the teens could let loose and develop their own personal movement styles, inspired by the spirited gyrating of the pioneering rock 'n' roll performers.

Slow Dancing

The dancing that the teens did to the slow rock 'n' roll songs of the 1950s was hardly dancing at all. The "dance" they performed was ostensibly a version of the Slow Foxtrot, a dance that earlier generations had done to leisurely pop arrangements that was sometimes called "music to hug by."[31] However, the Fifties teens eventually did away with almost all of the Foxtrot's traveling figures and foot patterns. They simply stood in place, holding tight to their partner, and gently swayed or stepped back and forth or around in a circle. The main idea was to luxuriate in as much physical body-to-body contact as your partner, the dance's chaperones, or the behavioral codes of the time and place would allow. At a sock hop, a slow song would generally be played at the very end of the evening and it was reserved for a partner with whom one had a special, romantic relationship.

Fifties teens also did a risqué version of slow dancing, known as the Fish. According to American social-dance chronicler Ralph Giordano, the Fish was actually an updated version of a dance from the early 1900s, the Slow Drag, in which couples hung onto one another and would just grind back and forth in one spot all night. Movements for the Slow Drag were codified in 1911 by ragtime composer Scott Joplin, who described steps for the dance on the sheet music for his song "Treemonisha." He suggested taking a step on the first beat of each measure of the music. When stepping forward, the dancer was to then drag the left foot. When stepping back, it was the right foot that would be dragged. Moving sideways to the right, the dancer would drag the left foot, and moving sideways to the left, the dancer would drag the right foot. Joplin also described variations of the dance involving prancing, marching, sliding, hopping, and skipping steps. It is unlikely, however, that these more lively variations were practiced, as they run counter to the kinesthetic dynamics and kind of close, sensual partner work associated with slow dancing. The Fish had no designated step patterns whatsoever. When dancing it, the male would simply concentrate on trying to slowly grind his pelvis against the thigh of his female partner.[32]

Paralleling the tightly choreographed, unison movements performed by the rock 'n' roll vocal groups popular in the 1950s, an assortment of choreographed group dances constructed of simple stylized actions emerged during the latter part of the decade. The dances were performed independently, yet in a group formation. And while the dances were sometimes done in couples, partners generally made no physical contact, though they may have stood face to face, side by side, or across from one another in the group set-up. With their allowance for independence within a social environment, and their emphasis on synchronized action, these dances mirrored, and no doubt gratified, the conflicting desires that plague most youngsters during their teenage years. Adolescents can often be psychologically conflicted as they struggle to balance their wish to establish independence from their parents, with the simultaneous need to "fit in" and feel a sense of belonging with their peers.

Large groups of performers dancing together in perfect unison, such as chorus lines and drill teams, have always been a popular form of American theatrical entertainment. But while teens' performance of such highly synchronized dances in a social setting can be seen to reflect the peer pressure to conform felt by most adolescents, their execution of group dances in the 1950s can also be viewed as a clue to the larger societal climate of the times, a period characterized, at least on the surface, by conformist sensibilities.

The 1950s was a time of economic abundance and feelings of great security for most Americans, but those comforts brought with them a requisite conformity that many would ultimately find stifling. In the prosperity of the '50s, huge numbers of people could afford to buy single homes in middle-class suburbs. But those houses—famously exemplified by the Levittown housing developments on New York's Long Island and in Bucks County, Pennsylvania—all looked alike. The sameness of the design was, in large part, what allowed the homes to be built so quickly and cheaply. Well-paying jobs with big businesses were increasingly available to the new suburbanites, but an unwavering dedication to the company and a "team player" mindset were strictly demanded of the 1950s corporate businessman. One of the most insightful books of the period was Sloan Wilson's 1955 novel *The Man in the Grey Flannel Suit*, a telling portrayal of a businessman's struggles against the conformist pressures of the era. And while America may have been stopping the spread of Communism, both through the Cold War abroad and at home with the persecution of perceived Communist-leaning Americans by Senator Joseph McCarthy, the price paid by U.S. citizens was the repression of any expression of "un-American" political opinions and the forced proclamation of support for commonly held values. Regardless of one's individual political beliefs, it was not unusual during the 1950s for Americans to have to sign loyalty oaths professing their rejection of Communism in order to get or maintain jobs. The strictly choreographed rock 'n' roll dances of the 1950s, therefore, can be viewed as a reflection of the era's pervasive conformity, the need to reinforce the value and necessity of an assimilated population, with shared attitudes, working together toward common goals.

Hand Jive

The most clear-cut example of the synchronized, choreographed dances practiced by the Fifties teens, and perhaps the easiest to execute, is the Hand Jive. The dance requires very little space and can be performed by a group of people sitting close together, such as on bleachers in a gymnasium. The Hand Jive can also be done standing up, facing a partner. If done standing, it is best to assume a slightly hunched-over, bent-knee position so that your thighs and shoulders are in relatively close proximity. Such positioning makes it easier for the dancer to perform the requisite movements at a quick pace.

The Hand Jive consists of a series of small, gestural actions, performed in a steady rhythm, with each move falling directly on the beat of the music. It begins with both hands slapping twice on the thighs, clapping twice, and then making slicing actions, twice with the right hand cutting over the left, and twice with left over right. The hands next form fists as the left pounds twice atop the right, followed by the right pounding twice upon the left. The right thumb is then extended and aimed twice over the right shoulder (as if hitch-hiking), followed by the same movement with the left thumb. The entire sequence is then repeated as many times as desired. Variations of the dance may insert turning, jumping, or other kinds of movements as breaks in between the basic sequence of hand choreography.

Published instructions for the Hand Jive often direct dancers to do the slicing and fist-pounding actions first with the right hand on top. However, if it is important that the "hitch-hiking" gesture be done first with the right thumb, natural kinesthetic logic would dictate putting the left hand on top first when doing the fist-pounding movement. That way the right fist ends up on top and has a clear pathway to the shoulder. It can then move easily into the thumb action, rather than having to awkwardly sneak out from underneath the other fist when it comes time to "hitch-hike." As the hitch-hiking gesture is the largest and most choreographically interesting movement of the sequence, it is best to set up the action so as to support the strongest execution of that step. Particularly for non-professional dancers, movements that are physically natural are generally the easiest to perform well. Moreover, as the left hand winds up on top at the end of the slicing movements, keeping it in that position and starting the pounding action with the left fist on top makes for a smoother, more natural transition.

The Hand Jive enjoyed its greatest popularity during the summer of 1958. It was danced to the Johnny Otis song "Willie and the Hand Jive." If there was any significance behind the creation of the dance, other than the desire to invent a fun novelty activity, the driving force was probably two-fold. First, there is the notion that it is impossible not to perform some sort of movement when listening to a rock 'n' roll song. Even if you are not out on the dance floor, the music, nonetheless, "compels" you to dance. Thus, the Hand Jive affords you the opportunity to do so, even if your hands are the only body parts you have room to move. Second, the highly choreographed Hand Jive allows all teens to feel as though they are part of a communal dance activity, even those who do not have a partner, did not get asked to dance, or for whom there is simply no room out on the floor. An elaborate Hand Jive dance number can be seen in the 1978 hit movie *Grease* (see chapter 5).

The Madison

The most intricate of the era's choreographed group dances was the late-1950s fad dance, The Madison. It is generally agreed that The Madison was originated by African Americans in the Midwest and eventually appropriated by white teens nationwide. Some say the dance was first performed in Detroit, and others place its origins in Indiana. But the only story that accounts for why the dance is called The Madison and why it begins with the left foot (which is atypical in group choreography) is that reported in an Ohio newspaper in 1960.[33] According to that account, the dance was invented at a black social club in Columbus, Ohio, in late 1957, by dancers under the mentorship of William "Bubbles" Holloway. It seems that Holloway had just returned from a trip to New York City, where he had asked for directions to Madison Avenue and was told to "take it to the left." When he returned home he recalled that phrase and used it as the basis for the development of a new dance that began on the left foot and which he named "The Madison." The dance quickly spread throughout Columbus and beyond, as Holloway took a team of dancers to

Atlantic City and then to Cleveland, where they demonstrated the new dance. Record producers hurried to put out recordings to accompany The Madison, one of which featured calls (see below) by Baltimore disc jockey Eddie Morrison, who helped popularize the dance by teaching it to teens who performed it on the Baltimore television dance program *The Buddy Deane Show* (see chapter 3).

The Madison was generally done in parallel, horizontal lines, with everyone facing forward when performed in settings where there was any sort of audience. At private parties, however, it was sometimes executed in a circle. Done to music with a 4/4 meter, the dance features a six-count basic step that is interspersed with idiosyncratically named variations that are performed in response to the commands of a caller, like in an American Square Dance. The basic step includes six distinct movements, each done on one beat of the music: a touch of the left foot as it reaches diagonally across the right, a touch of the left foot out to the left side, another touch of the left foot diagonally across the right, a step forward on the left, a touch of the right foot directly next to the left, and a backward step on the right. Hand claps or finger snaps are sometimes added on the fifth count.

The variations are slightly longer phrases that include novelty movements representative of letters, sports and entertainment figures, or character types. For example "The Jackie Gleason" (or "Away We Go") variation involves the execution of three movements of the same foot—a forward brush, a cutting action in which the foot ends up crossed in front of the other ankle, and a low kick out to the side—just like Gleason would do in his signature sign-off movement. The move is often described as resembling the tap step known as "Shuffle Off to Buffalo" because the second of its three distinct movements, the cutting across action, puts the legs into the signature "numeral 4" shape contained in the Buffalo. Also, Gleason's use of the step as an impetus for his departure reflects the Buffalo's origins as a traveling step that vaudeville-era dancers used to exit the stage.[34]

Reflecting the popularity of western novels, movies, and television programs at the time—1959 was the peak year for TV westerns—a variation called "The Rifleman" includes three hopping steps and the pantomiming of holding, lifting, and shooting a gun. And a "Cowboys and Indians" variation incorporates the miming of pistol shooting. Other variations include the "Big M," in which the dancer takes steps that form a letter "M," "Make a T," which uses a jumping-jack movement to symbolize the making of the letter, and sequences with names such as Two Up and Two Back, the Big Boss, the Box, Cuddle Me, and Flying High. Additional variations honor the legendary basketball player Wilt Chamberlain and quarterback Johnny Unitas with movements that resemble hook shots and forward passes.[35]

While the caller on the record indicates to The Madison dancers when they are to start ("Hit it") and stop ("Erase it") a particular variation, the calls do not provide specific instructions on how to do the basic step or any of the variations. The dancers had to have learned the steps ahead of time and become familiar with all of the named variations. While the moves were not physically challenging, they were too intricate to pick up on the spot. The Madison, therefore, was not a dance that allowed for spontaneous participation or improvisation. Rather than providing an outlet for adolescent tensions, it served more to gratify the youth culture's need for communal experience and to underline conformist values. Music professor Tim Wall described the dance as "a communal and individual display of cultural competence achieved, in part, through a mastery of the figures, the

Cast members of the 2002 Broadway musical *Hairspray* dancing The Madison. (Joan Marcus/Photofest)

unconventional timing, the knowledge of the cultural references in the narration, and their interpretation as stylized movement imbued with the insolence and understated swagger of youth."[36] A large group demonstration of The Madison is featured in the 1988 film *Hairspray* (see chapter 5).

As the decade wore on and rock 'n' roll music continued to surge in popularity, new dances were invented, quickly popularized, and, for the most part, tolerated by adults. Rock 'n' roll dancing also started to lose some of its regional diversity as teenagers all over the country were suddenly dancing the same dances at the same time and in similar fashion. All of these dramatic changes—the creation of new dances, their national dissemination, and the decline of parental opposition—were the result of one transforming force: television.

Just as radio had fueled the rock 'n' roll music explosion, television catalyzed the further evolution and wider acceptance of rock 'n' roll dancing. With the introduction of some clever choreographic innovations, a sanitized image of teens, and the incorporation of competitive and soap opera-like elements, a new kind of television show emerged that changed the course of rock 'n' roll history. The prototype was *American Bandstand,* a landmark program that enjoyed unprecedented popularity and proved that teenagers dancing to rock 'n' roll music could make for riveting, socially acceptable entertainment. What is its story?

3

Teenage Terps on Television

If Philadelphians had had a more voracious appetite for old English movies, *American Bandstand*—the most influential force in rock 'n' roll dancing of the 1950s—might never have happened. Roger Clipp, the station manager of Philadelphia's WFIL-TV, a local ABC affiliate, was looking to create a new program in the early 1950s to replace the station's daily afternoon showings of old English films, which were drawing a very small number of viewers. Clipp was eager for the new program to make use of the several thousand dollars worth of short films of musical performances that the outlet had been talked into buying and which had come to be known around the station as "WFIL's folly." Clipp envisioned a program formed by stringing together the showing of these cinematic acquisitions, which were a collection of "Snaders" and films produced by Jimmy Roosevelt, son of President Franklin D. Roosevelt.[1]

Snaders was the informal term for Snader Telescriptions, which were three-minute films produced in the early 1950s by Louis D. Snader. Made to be shown on television, Snaders documented live musical performances by classical and popular artists. The Jimmy Roosevelt films were acquired from the movie distributor Official Films and were likely to have been "Soundies."[2] A film executive with Samuel Goldwyn Productions in the late 1930s, Jimmy Roosevelt founded his own film company, Globe Productions, around 1940.[3] His company partnered with the manufacturer of the Panoram, a

"motion picture-jukebox" that played short films of musical entertainment. Roosevelt's company produced those films, which were
called "Soundies," and are considered a precursor of the popular music videos birthed in the 1980s. Supposedly the most contemporary
performer featured in WFIL's lot of Roosevelt's films was the jazz
pianist Fats Waller, a popular entertainer of the 1930s. The Snaders,
on the other hand, included performances by famous 1950s pop singers, such as Peggy Lee and Nat King Cole.

Bob Horn's Bandstand

To host the new afternoon TV program, the station chose Bob Horn, a
popular DJ who was then hosting a successful music show on WFIL
radio, yet was yearning to break into television, which he perceived
as the entertainment industry's "wave of the future." Since Horn's
radio show had been called *Bob Horn's Bandstand*, the name *Bandstand*
was kept for the new TV program, which debuted in September 1952
and was produced by Tony Mammarella. The first show opened with
Horn seated at a table where he conducted an interview with the
trailblazing bebop trumpeter Dizzy Gillespie, followed by a Snader
of Peggy Lee singing "Manana."[4]

From the get-go, Horn knew that his show stank, but he was convinced that success could be had by bringing the elements that made
radio shows popular—music and talk—to television. What he was
missing, however, was a consideration of TV's essential aspect: its visual component. And as dance artists have known for centuries, one
of the most powerful ways to enhance visual expression is through
the addition of a kinesthetic element, that of human bodies in motion.
Watching other people's movements, particularly those designed in
meaningful relationships to one another, is of infinite interest to most
people and makes for unusually compelling entertainment. Moving bodies evoke a form of kinesthetic communication in which the
viewer experiences actual physical responses in empathetic reaction
to the motions made by or upon the bodies one is watching. It is like
the pain you feel in your own gut when you watch someone else get
punched in the stomach.

Horn and the studio executives soon hit on the notion of adding
dancing teenagers to the *Bandstand* program. They got the idea from
The 950 Club, then one of the most widely listened to radio shows

in Philadelphia. Airing on WPEN, and named for the station's position at 950 on the AM dial, the show was hosted by Joe Grady and Ed Hurst, who invited local teens to stop by the studio after school, when the show was on the air, and dance to the latest pop records. Sometimes the teens were asked to introduce themselves to the listening audience and talk about the high school they attended.

The 950 Club model was adopted to boost Horn's ailing *Bandstand*, the new format for which also included the addition of a co-host, Lee Stewart. Unsure of the show's potential, wary station executives insisted on hiring Stewart, since he came with a guaranteed sponsor, Muntz TV, a company for which Stewart appeared in television commercials as a wacky character known as "Mad Man Muntz." Stewart was also brought onboard with the idea that he and Horn could emulate the entertaining two-man banter of Grady and Hurst, of "The 950 Club." But it was the brilliantly simple concept of the dancing teens that was responsible for transforming *Bandstand* from a stodgy films-and-interviews program to a trendsetting rock 'n' roll music and dance show that would eventually capture the attention of the entire country.

More than 1,000 teens showed up to dance on *Bandstand* when it premiered in its new format on October 7, 1952. But since only about 200 could fit into the studio, the rest remained lined up outside, and Horn showed a Snader every half-hour or so to give them time to rotate in a new group. With the new format—which also involved the addition of live appearances by top musical artists lip-synching to their hit records, as well as dance contests and record-rating by the teens—the show's popularity skyrocketed. Broadcast live five days a week during the after-school hours, *Bandstand* became one of the most watched programs in the city. Though its hosts were originally intended to work as a comedy team—with Stewart as the funny guy and Horn the straight man—their personalities never clicked. By 1955, when the show had become so successful that the station no longer needed to worry about attracting sponsors, Stewart was let go and Horn hosted the show alone.[5]

In the summer of 1956, Horn was arrested for driving while under the influence of alcohol. Though such irresponsible behavior on the part of the host of a show for youngsters would alone have been cause for concern, in this instance it was especially embarrassing to the station, as the company that owned WFIL also owned the *Philadelphia*

Inquirer, which was in the process of promoting an aggressive campaign against drunk driving. Horn was fired immediately. Upon his dismissal, *Bandstand's* producer temporarily filled in as host of the show. Soon, however, the position was taken over by a clean-cut, 26-year-old, ambitious DJ, Dick Clark, who had been hosting a music show on WFIL radio. Clark would continue to host some version of *Bandstand* for the next 30 years, as his name and persona grew virtually synonymous with the promotion and presentation of rock 'n' roll in America.

When Horn was let go from his position as host, some of the *Bandstand* teens got very upset and protested with picket signs outside the WFIL studios. Many other teens, however, were so eager to dance on the show that they genially made the transition to working with Clark. There were even others who did not miss Horn at all. He had a rather gruff personality and made little attempt to relate to the kids. One teenager who danced on Horn's *Bandstand* described him as "grumpy" and insincere, noting that his off-camera personality was considerably less charming than the more pleasant manner he adopted when on the air.[6]

Most of the teens who danced frequently on the show came from one of the three large high schools that were located close by the studios: West Catholic High School for Girls, West Catholic High School for Boys, and the public West Philadelphia High School. While the teens were essentially all white, there was an "ethnic" quality to the show, as it seemed to attract a disproportionate number of Italian-American teenagers from the working class neighborhoods of South Philadelphia.

On any given day, there were many more teens who wanted to dance on *Bandstand* than could fit in the studio. The teens had to race over quickly from school and wait in line to be selected, in what was essentially a first-come-first-serve system, which is why those from the closest schools were most often picked. However, there also developed a system of "regulars" that was known as "The Committee." These were teens who had been given special membership cards that allowed them to move immediately to the front of the line and get on the show virtually anytime they wanted. There even developed a sub-system, whereby the regulars had the authority to bring friends to the front of the line and into the studio with them.

Teenagers lined up outside the television studio in Philadelphia, hoping to get on the teen dance program *American Bandstand*, circa 1959. (Temple University Libraries, Urban Archives, Philadelphia, PA)

Bandstand was broadcast from the WFIL studios at 46th and Market Streets, just across from The Arena, the city's 4,000-seat sports and concert stadium, and in a neighborhood populated almost equally by blacks and working-class whites. From its inception, the show had always featured many African-American musical artists as guest performers. Nonetheless, one of the most common criticisms leveled against *Bandstand* during the 1950s was that until 1957 it was, albeit unofficially, a whites-only show in terms of its teenage participants. And even after that, while black teens were not prohibited from appearing on the show, they were rarely seen on-camera, and were not allowed to dance with white partners.[7] Their slim visibility on *Bandstand* was grossly out of proportion to their significant presence as residents of the neighborhood where the WFIL studios were located. Even though teenagers were demonstrating new notions of racial relationships with their rock 'n' roll music preferences and dancing behaviors, the segregated nature of *Bandstand* is a clear reminder that the 1950s was an era when the values of an older order still governed the workings of societal and commercial institutions.

Dick Clark's *American Bandstand*

An astute businessman who went on to become one of the most financially successful producers in the American entertainment industry, the entrepreneurial Clark began making fervent pitches to the ABC executives in New York, urging them to pick up his local *Bandstand* program as a network show and broadcast it nationwide. In less than 13 months, Clark got his way.

When it was decided that *Bandstand* was to go national, a few alterations were immediately made. First, the name of the show was changed from *Bandstand* to *American Bandstand*. Second, it was decided that when the teens introduced themselves they would no longer say the name of their high school, just their own name and their age. And third, the set was re-designed. The painted, canvas record-store backdrop and counter were replaced by a field of gold records hung in gold-trimmed frames. Clark stood in front of the records, up on a riser, behind a podium. The kids sat on pine, pull-out, gymnasium-style bleachers, which were off to Clark's right, along with a table at which the musical artists would sit and sign autographs. On the far wall were three windows: one into the Control Room, another for sponsors to watch from, and a third that opened into the studio executives' offices. The dance area was directly in front of Clark, and to his left was a big, glittery-edged, cutout map of the United States, inside of which a floor full of teens would appear dancing at the opening of each show. There was a broken red line on the dance floor: one side designated the dancing space, while the other was the camera area. The producer would fight to keep the kids on their side of the line, as they would often move up close to it, jockeying for position in front of the cameras.[8] If the dance floor never looked uncomfortably crowded on television, it was probably due to the skills of the cameramen. Pat Shook, a teen who danced on *Bandstand* in the early years, recalls being shocked when she entered the studio for the first time and saw how small the floor was. "We were bumper-to-bumper in there," she said.[9]

On August 5, 1957, *American Bandstand* made its national network debut, airing on 67 stations coast to coast. It quickly became "the" show that teens all across America raced home to watch in order to keep abreast of the latest rock 'n' roll records, to see what dances were being done to the songs, and to emulate the fashions in clothing and hairdos that the teens on *Bandstand* were exhibiting. Within just a few weeks of going national, the show was receiving about 15,000 weekly fan letters and was reaching more viewers than any other program on daytime television.[10]

Along with the dancing teens and the lip-synched performances by the rock 'n' roll stars, the show also featured a popular interactive element: dance contests. Largely just a ploy to generate more fan mail, specific dance contests were set up in which the regulars would all do a particular dance and viewers would write in voting for their favorites. Within a normal week, *American Bandstand* would usually receive about 45,000 pieces of mail, while during a contest week it could get close to 150,000.[11] In the opinion of Arlene Sullivan, one of the most famous *American Bandstand* regulars, the dance competitions had very little to do with dance ability. "They were really just popularity contests. The most popular couple always won first prize," she said.[12]

Another popular feature of *American Bandstand* was the special segment called "Record Review." (In the 1960s it was re-named "Rate-A-Record.") Three teens would be chosen to listen to and numerically rate three new records. The teens could rate each record with a number from 35 (the worst) to 98 (the best). A fourth teen would be charged with the task of calculating the average score for each record, which would then be posted on a board on the studio wall. When the teens liked a record and were going to give it a high rating, they would often say something to the effect of, "It's got a great beat, and you can dance to it. I'll give it a . . ." Because of how often the teens used those, or very similar, words, the phrase "It's got a great beat, and you can dance to it" has become immortalized as a symbol of *American Bandstand*. Simply say those words to anyone who was alive and old enough to watch TV during the 1950s and they will know exactly what you are talking about. As a reward for participating in the Record Review, the teens were always given some sort of gift. A teen who got picked to rate the records one day in December 1957 recalled receiving a recording of the iconic Philadelphia newscaster John Facenda reading "The Nativity" and a copy of Elvis Presley's Christmas album as his gift.[13]

Typically, the *Bandstand* teens were quite accurate in their ratings and gave high scores to many recordings that went on to be big hits. On one occasion, however, they were embarrassingly wrong. It was 1963, and the teens were rating a recording of "She Loves You" by the Beatles. They gave it an average score of just 73—a relative flop on the *Bandstand* scale—and laughed when they were shown a photograph of the long-haired English foursome who sang it.[14] Who knew that the Beatles were soon to take off as one of the greatest forces in rock 'n' roll history?

Because *American Bandstand* was broadcast every weekday, audiences grew very familiar with the show's regular teenage participants and wrote letters asking about their personal lives. For example, most of the show's regulars danced with the same partner all the time, and fans wanted to know if the couples were boyfriend-girlfriend and obsessively followed the ups and downs of their romantic relationships. It was for this exact reason that the Committee of regulars was established, so that viewers could develop a familiarity and sense of identification with the kids. The show's producers knew that the program needed a continuity that would make spectators continue to tune in every day. Though they were just average teens, with no special talents other than some innate dance ability, the *American Bandstand* regulars quickly became national "stars." They were written about in teen magazines, had fan clubs established in their honor, and would typically receive several hundred fans letters a week.[15]

The importance of *American Bandstand* for teenage America extended beyond just entertainment. Social-dance historian Julie Malnig, who has conducted extensive research on televised teen dance programs, stresses how teens' observation of dancing by other teens, with whom they closely identified, helped develop "a sense of community, security, and familiarity" among the youth culture of the 1950s. It "drew them into a 'virtual' community of dancers with whom they could take vicarious pleasure." Watching other teens dancing on TV, which they might have done alone and perhaps in defiance of their parents, also played to the teenager's inherent conflict between rebellion and conformity. It allowed them to be alone, yet still together.[16]

The dancers on *American Bandstand* had to be between the ages of 14 and 18: 13-year-olds could be too giddy, and prohibiting anyone over 18 kept out military personnel. It was thought that the sight of their young daughter dancing on TV with a soldier or sailor she had

Clean-cut teenagers dancing on TV's mega-hit show *American Bandstand*, hosted by Dick Clark. It was by watching this program that teens nationwide kept abreast of the latest trends in rock 'n' roll dancing of the 1950s. (ABC/Photofest)

just met might prove threatening to any number of parents. The show also maintained a specified dress code and behavioral rules that got more stringent when the show went national. The teens wore what would then have been called "school clothes." Boys were required to wear a dress shirt, neat pants, and a jacket or a sweater and tie. Girls had to wear dresses or skirts and were not permitted to wear pants or sweaters that were too tight-fitting. Gum-chewing was verboten.

Because of the vast influence the *American Bandstand* dancers had on setting fashion trends among the teenagers of the late 1950s, there developed an interest among fashion-conscious young girls all over the country in a new style they referred to as the "Philadelphia collar." But unbeknownst to the teens who wanted to emulate the style, its origins were completely inadvertent. Many of the girls who danced on *American Bandstand* came from the neighboring Catholic high school, where the administration did not approve of their students appearing on national television dancing to rock 'n' roll music. "The Catholic schools were very prudish then and frowned on us dancing on *Bandstand*. They thought it was lewd," said Jack Gunod, a Catholic schoolboy who danced on the show.[17] While their objections were in large part rooted in the church's stance against rock 'n' roll and its "immoral" influences, the school officials also claimed that the desire to dance on *Bandstand* was prompting students to leave school early so as to be guaranteed a place at the front of the line. Since they could not legally prevent their pupils from appearing on *Bandstand,* the school instituted a policy that forbade any West Catholic High School students from appearing on *Bandstand* wearing their school uniform. Yet how could the girls find time to change their clothes, and still get to the studio on time, while not breaking the school's rule concerning leaving early? They couldn't. Their solution was to bring a sweater or some sort of top with them that they would quickly throw on to cover their school uniform. What generally happened is that the collar of the blouse they wore as part of their school attire would stick out over the neckline of the sweater. With so many girls on the show sporting this "fashion," teens watching from outside Philadelphia assumed it to be the latest trend in collar styles. Girls all over the country suddenly began inquiring as to where they could buy blouses that had that Philadelphia collar.

In addition to the trends it set in fashion, music, dance, and teenage behavior, *American Bandstand* popularized the idea that audiences can digest music through a visual medium. This idea influenced not only the development of popular music, but also the evolution of television as a conveyor of musical performance. A continuum can be traced all the way from *American Bandstand* to the innovative music videos that revolutionized the pop music industry in the 1980s.[18] The show was also a prototype in the development of reality TV. A precursor to the countless reality shows that 40 years later constituted the most popular "new" genre of television programming, *American Bandstand* exhibited virtually all of the elements that characterize reality TV: the voyeuristic viewing of ordinary people, competitive contests, and the soap opera-like drama that is woven out of the personal lives of those who appear on the show. Also, like most reality programs, *American Bandstand* did not need to employ professional actors, writers, costume and scenic designers, or hair and make-up artists on any kind of regular basis. It is because they save on these kinds of expenditures that reality shows can be produced so inexpensively, thus their great appeal to the television networks and independent producers.

But perhaps the most pervasive influence exerted by *American Bandstand* is the change it caused in the perception of rock 'n' roll among the population at large. Whereas during the initial years of the show the teens danced largely to popular music of the same ilk that their parents might have listened to, by the time the show went national rock 'n' roll had become the teenagers' music and it was mainly to rock 'n' roll records that the youth danced on *American Bandstand*. Seeing a controlled group of ordinary, polite, well-dressed, largely white teenagers dancing joyfully to rock 'n' roll did a lot to alter people's opinion of the music. Dick Clark also played an extremely important role in this laundering of rock 'n' roll's image. A debonair adult presence, with a boy-next-door quality, and youthful enough for the kids to relate to, Clark made parents comfortable with the idea of teens getting together and dancing to rock 'n' roll. Clark was also very image-conscious in the selection of musical artists whom he invited to appear on his show. Despite his status as an inventor of rock 'n' roll, Jerry Lee Lewis found all his future bookings on *American Bandstand* cancelled by Clark when it was announced, to much public outrage, that Lewis had married his 13-year-old cousin.[19]

Yet for all he did to promote rock 'n' roll, Clark himself never danced to rock 'n' roll music. He thought himself to be a very poor dancer. Ironically, when Clark was growing up in Mt. Vernon, New York, his family's next-door neighbor was Arthur Murray. With his chain of franchised ballroom-dance studios that proliferated during the 1950s, his is perhaps the most famous name in the world of dance instruction. Though Clark never felt comfortable participating in rock 'n' roll dancing, as a youth he was given a free set of ballroom dance lessons by Murray. "I can still cut a mean Foxtrot," Clark wrote in his 1978 book *Rock, Roll and Remember*.

Dancing Philly Style

Prior to *American Bandstand*'s emergence as a national television show, the kind of dancing that teens did to rock 'n' roll varied from place to place and was based largely on personal adaptations of the Swing-era Jitterbug. *American Bandstand* brought a large degree of homogeneity to the practice of rock 'n' roll dancing and placed a prominence on what could be described as the Philadelphia style of dancing. According to Ray Smith, a dancer who appeared frequently on *Bandstand* from 1956 to 1959, the primary dance done on the show during that period was the Jitterbug. However, Philadelphians had a distinctive way of dancing the Jitterbug that was cooler, smoother, and more restrained than how it was danced elsewhere. "The thing about Philadelphia-style dancing is that it's very tight. You're always pulling in. In a sense it's very 'black,' very understated, very 'cool.' You don't move wildly all over the place, or with a sense of reaching up and out, everything is down. It's as if there's a constant rhythm that pulses through your hips and down your legs," explained Smith.[20]

The popular *American Bandstand* regular Arlene Sullivan agrees that there is a distinct Philadelphia Jitterbug style, but also notes that the style differed from one neighborhood of the city to another. "You would dance with guys from different parts of the city and they'd dance differently. The guys from South Philly did more pausing, less turning of the girls, more just fast moving of the feet. The North Philly guys did more twisting of the arms. And the guys from Norristown [a Philadelphia suburb] would put their two hands together and do a kind of push that was very different from what we did in the city. So the girls were the ones who were really good because we had to follow these boys with all their different styles," said Sullivan.[21]

In addition to exhibiting their own dancing styles, the Philadelphians on *American Bandstand* also introduced the country to many new dances that became Fifties fads. The first 1950s dance that was claimed to have been created or at least popularized by the *Bandstand* dancers was not a rock 'n' roll dance, as it pre-dates the emergence of rock 'n' roll music. It was the Bunny Hop, invented in 1952 to go with a new recording by big band leader Ray Anthony.[22]

During *Bandstand*'s Bob Horn era, the head of the Committee of regulars was Jerry Blavat, who was considered the best male dancer on the show. In loyalty to Horn, Blavat left *Bandstand* when its original host was dismissed, but went on to become one of Philadelphia's leading DJs and the force behind the creation of many popular line dances of the 1960s. Blavat feels there existed a special creativity among the *Bandstand* dancers that was unique to Philadelphia and was lost when Clark moved the show to Los Angeles, in 1964. "Out there the kids did the same dance to every record," Blavat opined.[23]

Ray Smith feels that the reason there was such enormous creative activity going on among the *Bandstand* dancers was because of the pressure to come up with something different to do each day to the new songs. "You had to be creative. You knew people were watching and if you did the same thing all the time the show would be boring," he explained. Mindful of the need to keep viewers interested throughout the show's lengthy time slot (which varied over the years, and in different locales, from an hour to two-and-a-half hours), Clark would play a wide variety of music. The teens were expected to come up with something on the spot that would be suitable to dance to each different record. "That was the fun of it," said Smith, who also claims that when *American Bandstand* was broadcast from Philadelphia, the kind of dancing exhibited on the show was a true reflection of how ordinary teenagers of the period danced. Whereas when the show moved to California, "it became show biz kids, performing for the camera," he said.[24]

Just because so many new dances were introduced on *Bandstand*, it is not correct to assume that those dances were all created by the *Bandstand* teens. Many people claim that the white *Bandstand* dancers got a lot of their ideas for new moves, steps, and styles from watching their black peers.[25] While African-American teens could be observed dancing at school, record hops, or parties, the most widely visible platform for the showcasing of black teen dancing in the Philadelphia area was *The Mitch Thomas Show.* Described by some as "the black *Bandstand*," the show was a local television teen-dance program, much like *American Bandstand* in format, except that the participants were all black. Broadcast in the late 1950s, originally from Wilmington, Delaware, and then from a studio atop Suburban Station in center-city Philadelphia, the show was named after its host, Mitch Thomas. Featuring the latest in African-American dance styles, it was considered an important source for learning new dance steps.

According to Moe Booker, who was one of the members of *The Mitch Thomas Show's* equivalent of *Bandstand's* Committee of regulars, "some of those same kids that would go on *Bandstand* would come to *The Mitch Thomas Show* and watch the dances. . . . And so, consequently, many of the dances that black kids had had a great deal to do with made their way onto the *Bandstand* show."[26] Even though to most viewers *American Bandstand* may have appeared to be a white-oriented operation, a close, informed, and analytical look at the show's dancing teens reveals an important way in which black influences were being infused into mainstream American culture in the 1950s.

In 1959, the teenagers Jimmy Peatross and Joan Buck introduced a new dance on *American Bandstand* called the Strand. A graceful, spinning dance with lots of smooth, close, and intricate partner-work, the Strand proved extremely difficult for most people to do. When on the air one day Clark asked Peatross and Buck where they had learned the dance, they said they made it up. In reality, they had not originated the dance, but had seen it being done by their African-American high school classmates. Despite its complexity, Buck and Peatross managed to copy and perform it very well. They later admitted that Clark caught them off-guard with his question and they only lied about making up the Strand because they were afraid they would have been frowned upon if they had said they had learned it from blacks.[27]

Not only was *American Bandstand* responsible for manufacturing many of the '50s dance fads, but it also served as an important "teacher" of the dances to kids all across the country. Sharon Decker, a '50s teen who grew up in a small farming town outside Madison, Wisconsin, said, "We watched it every afternoon as soon as we got home from school. That's how we learned to dance."[28] Dave Frees, director of the *American Bandstand* fan club, recalled how he employed the refrigerator door as his partner while he got his daily "private dance lesson" from the show. "[The door] was just the right weight, not too heavy but not as light and flimsy-feeling as say, a broomstick, and it had this nice smooth motion on its hinges, and you could pull it out and let it swing back, and almost close and then catch it, like you were spinning your partner in a Jitterbug."[29]

Sensitive to the show's role as an "at-home dance class" for the nation's teens, the *Bandstand* cameramen spent a lot of time focusing in tightly on the dancers' feet, making it easier for viewers to pick up the steps and to see exactly how the new dances were done. So important was the "educational" camera-work—being able to capture the dances close-up and from varying perspectives—that *American Bandstand* was one of the last network television programs to switch from black and white to color. In the late 1950s, color television cameras were quite large and immobile. Only one color camera would have been able to fit into the small studio from which *American Bandstand* was broadcast and it would not have been able to move around very much. The use of multiple, mobile cameras was felt to be of central importance to the mission of the show, so it was not until 1967 that *American Bandstand* was presented in color.[30]

The Bop

The first new rock 'n' roll dance to be introduced on *American Bandstand* was the Bop, presented in the summer of 1957. The Bop was a dance from southern California that was being done to the rockabilly classic "Be-Bop-A-Lula" by Gene Vincent and the Bluecaps. A couple of teenagers from California, who were in Philadelphia visiting relatives, had gotten onto *Bandstand* one day and started doing the Bop. (It was common for teens from all over the country to urge their parents to plan family trips to Philadelphia in the late 1950s so that they could try to appear on *American Bandstand*.) When Clark saw the California couple dancing the Bop in the studio, he asked to have the couple hang around after the show and teach their dance to the *American Bandstand* regulars.

Dancing the Bop entails jumping up and down as if on a pogo stick, and grinding your heels into the floor each time you land. It is done with a partner, yet not holding hands, because of the difficulty of doing so while jumping. The regulars found the dance exhausting, but learned it and performed it on the show nonetheless. The rest of the teenagers on the program imitated them, and within a week, all the *American Bandstand* dancers were doing the Bop. That fall Vincent released another Bop record, "Dance to the Bop," which became a big hit; its sales aided, no doubt, by the TV show's role in popularizing the dance.[31]

When songwriter Artie Singer approached Clark with a new dance tune, "Do the Bop," Clark told him that by the time the song got recorded and released the Bop dance fad would be over. Clark suggested that the song be re-named and the lyrics re-written to express what goes on at a record hop. To inspire the new lyrics, Clark conveyed some of the slang phrases he had heard the kids using, described what the current dances were like, and recalled typical record hop scenes. Singer took Clark's advice, and the song, recorded by Danny & the Juniors, went on to become the rock 'n' roll classic "At the Hop."[32]

The Bop that was done on *Bandstand* is not to be confused with the more generic term "Bop," which is used to describe a form of Lindy-based partner dance that has been done for many years by people of all ages in African-American communities. This Bop started during the bebop era of jazz music, in the 1940s, and was passed down from one generation to another. The emphasis is on the display of individual style or steps. Slightly different forms of the dance evolved in different regions, fueled in part by the competitive spirit of African-American dancers from different locales. For example, the Bop as danced in Baltimore was stylistically different from the Bop done in Washington, D.C., or Chicago. A dancer could be recognized as being a native of a particular area based on the way he danced the Bop.

The "Philly Bop," as it was practiced in North Philadelphia (which was different from the smoother, more conservative "West Philly Bop") consisted of a basic step—resembling the fundamental Jitterbug step—interspersed with breakaway sections during which the partners freely improvised their own movements. The partners stayed together musically during the breakaways by maintaining the common rhythm of the basic step. As the dance proceeded the couple transitioned seamlessly back and forth between unison executions of the basic step and the improvisational breakaway sections.[33] A white teen who grew up in the Midwest remembers a friend teaching her a dance that they referred to as the "Dirty Bop." "It was like the Jitterbug, but with no acrobatics, just lots of footwork, and you did it to very fast rock 'n' roll songs," she said.[34] Though originally performed by adults to jazz music, during the 1950s the Bop was done to rock 'n' roll, and continued to be danced afterwards to a variety of pop music genres.

A dancer was commonly taught the Bop by parents, siblings, aunts, uncles, or even grandparents. And it is from this dance that the term "teenybopper" is thought to be derived. According to oral folkloric history, an African-American youngster learning how to Bop was called a "teenybopper," well before the term came into mainstream usage as a general descriptor of adolescents.[35]

Two instructional dance publications from the mid-1950s—Johnny Sands's *How to Bop* and Art Silva's *How to Dance the Bop*—offer somewhat differing codified steps for the dance. But as the two stress the Bop's roots in earlier African-American vernacular dances and its strong improvisatory element, it is likely that they are both describing the generic Bop, not the fad dance performed on *American Bandstand*. Silva presents a basic step that involves lifting the heels on the off-beat and dropping them to the floor on the downbeat. Knee bends, torso tilts, and inward rotation of the legs are added to the foot action. Variations included a traveling step, a "scooter" move in which one leg is lifted while the other moves along the floor with a toe-heel pattern, and a whole series of Swing-dance partner work done with the basic Bop step. Silva claims that the dance's closest "relative" is the Charleston.

Sands calls the dance a composite of Charleston, Swing, Jitterbug, Boogie, and "the Negroe [*sic*] Shuffle." His descriptions of the Bop figures include a basic step he calls a "Roll-Rock" that involves shifting the body weight from heel to toe and variations based on inward and outward rotation of the legs, flicking motions of the feet, and a clapping action with the insides of the thighs, which he calls "Rubber Legs." Sands suggests that the dance originated in Texas in 1948.[36]

The Stroll

One of the most well-liked and pleasing to perform rock 'n' roll dances of the 1950s, the Stroll was another fad dance popularized on *American Bandstand*. Much less rigorous than the Bop, the Stroll was introduced on the show in 1957 by Chuck Willis. The Stroll had originally been revealed on *The Mitch Thomas Show* and was enjoying great popularity among Philadelphia's black community, where it was danced to Willis's rhythm and blues recording "C.C. Rider."

After the *American Bandstand* kids brought national attention to the dance, Clark once again played an advisory role in the development of a new record that surely profited from the publicity generated by his show. When the Canadian doo-wop quartet The Diamonds appeared on *American Bandstand* in November 1957, performing their single "Silhouettes," the group's manager saw the teens dancing the Stroll. Clark told the manager that it was a popular dance that needed a new song to go with it. The Diamonds immediately commissioned the writing of a song to fit the Stroll movements and by Christmas their recording of "The Stroll" was a top-selling record.[37]

Ideally performed with what has been described as "a calculated urban 'cool,'" the Stroll is a group dance done in two parallel lines, with the boys on one side and the girls on the other, facing each other like in a Virginia Reel.[38] The basic step of the Stroll is a 12-count movement phrase, which is actually a 6-count phrase simply repeated

The Stroll, danced by teens on *American Bandstand* in early 1958. Well-known program regular Arlene Sullivan appears on the far right. (Courtesy of the Library of Congress)

on the other side. The boys start the phrase with the left foot, the girls with the right. Beginning with the feet together, the phrase (on the boys' side) starts with a left diagonal touch forward (count 1) and then a touch of the left foot as it drags back into place next to the right (count 2). Next comes a forward diagonal step out onto the left (count 3), followed by a step onto the right as it cuts tightly behind the left (count 4). The phrase finishes with a step to the side with the left foot (count 5), and a touch, next to it, with the right (count 6). The entire sequence is then repeated starting with the right foot. It is the cutting-under action on count 4 that gives the otherwise pedestrian movement phrase its sense of style. It should be done with a slick quality and a sense of letting the cutting movement impel the knee of the opposite leg to bend as the heel lifts slightly. The addition of a sensual lean of the body as the weight is transferred lends another stylistic layer to the basic step.

The other essential element of the dance is the solo stroll by each couple. While the two lines of dancers perform the basic step, a couple formed from the boy and girl at the far end of the line (the end that is toward the boys' right and the girls' left) dances together down the aisle. The duo can take that opportunity to improvise movements of their own choosing or execute a forward traveling variation of the basic Stroll step. When the couple reaches the end of the lane, they split apart and replace the boy and girl at the end of the lines, as a new couple forms from the far end and begins their solo stroll. The nostalgic 1973 film *American Graffiti* (see chapter 5) features a scene at a sock hop in a school gymnasium, in which teenagers can be seen dancing the Stroll.

The Slop, the Walk, and the Circle Dance

Another distinctive '50s rock 'n' roll dance that originated in the African-American community was the Slop. Generally thought of as a "black" dance, it was not featured on *American Bandstand*. When dancing the Slop the men would put their hands in their pockets and yank up their pants legs as if showing off their shoes or their footwork. It was claimed that such action ensured that their pants did not drag along the floor or that they would not accidentally get their foot caught in their cuff. However, the gesture also lent a very distinctive style to one's dancing, which may have been the primary reason for doing it.[39] The Slop was performed to music of moderate tempo, and was done independently, without touching your partner. The movements of the Slop were sometimes incorporated into the improvised sections of the African-American Bop. While the Slop is generally considered a highly personalized, improvisatory dance, in Albert and Josephine Butler's exhaustive *Encyclopedia of Social Dance*, a codified description of the Slop is provided that includes a basic step featuring a shoulder dip and backward diagonal kick, as well as variations that involve swiveling on the balls of the feet and a "corkscrew round" done by crossing one foot behind the other and making a complete turn.

Unlike the Slop, the African-American dance known as the Walk was performed for a period on *American Bandstand*, though perhaps in a modified version from that originally done in the black community. The Walk was performed to a 1958 hit song of the same name by the jump blues singer Jimmy McCracklin. According to McCracklin, he made the record just to prove how easy it was to meet the simple taste of the rock 'n' roll audience. The success of his simple, repetitive record can be viewed as proof of his point.[40]

The Walk was done on *American Bandstand* in a Conga line–like formation, with the dancers one behind the other, holding on to the waist of the person in front of them. It traveled around the room with a two-action movement done first to one side then the other. The movement involved throwing out the same arm and leg, as the torso opened out to the side, and chugging forward slightly on the other leg as the working leg returned to its original position. The music has a heavy beat and a sloppy feel, which the style of the movement emulated. However, George Gray, one of the black male dancers featured on *The Mitch Thomas Show,* was known to be a master of the Walk. When he danced it his knees would bend out and in and he was described as looking "afflicted or deformed."[41]

Another short-lived dance fad, the Circle Dance, was invented on *American Bandstand* and can best be described as a kind of Square Dance figure done in the round. Three or four couples would stand in a big circle and one person would begin the dancing. "You'd push off the boy's arm and turn," recalls Arlene Sullivan, one of the *American Bandstand* regulars involved in the creation of the dance. The girl would then dance around the back of the circle, making hand contact with everyone along the way. When she got back to her original spot, the next person would take a turn dancing around the circle.[42]

The Cha-lypso and Rock Hybrid Dances

The most choreographically noteworthy dance invented on *American Bandstand* was the Cha-lypso, a combination of two popular partner dances: the Cha-Cha and the Calypso. The Cha-Cha emerged in the early 1950s as a simplified version of the Mambo. By adding a triple step in place of the Mambo's unnatural rest on the first beat of the measure, the Cha-Cha was much easier for beginning dancers to coordinate with the music. The Calypso is a sensual dance, characterized by rocking steps and gentle hip movements. The fusion of the two dances by the *American Bandstand* teens in 1957 resulted in a stylish new dance with solo turns and a swinging feel that could be done to a variety of different songs.

When first invented, the Cha-lypso was most commonly danced to Billy and Lillie's "La Dee Dah." However, when it became evident that the Cha-lypso would be around for a while, Clark stepped into his usual advisory role, nurturing the writing of new songs that would support the dances the teens did on his show. Clark suggested to songwriters Bob Crewe and Frank Slay that they write a fresh song for the cha-lypso. The result was "Lucky Ladybug," which Clark then played on his program every time he held a Cha-lypso contest.[43]

A host of other hybrid dances developed in the late 1950s that were terribly unimaginative dance-wise and are best viewed as reflections of the blatant commercialism that characterized the economically abundant decade. While some of the dances that had been invented to go with rock 'n' roll music may have sprung from genuinely creative impulses, the same cannot be said about most of the hybrid dances, which seemed to have been made simply as devices to sell records. In attempts to capitalize on teens' enthusiasm for anything "rock 'n' roll," familiar music and dances from the past were often re-made with a rock sound and presented as something brand new. It is important to remember that, unlike youngsters of earlier eras, the youth of the Fifties had significant buying power so many cultural trends were instigated for no other reason than the goal of capturing teen dollars.

In 1958, Dave Appell and the Applejacks scored a hit with "Mexican Hat Rock," an instrumental, rock 'n' roll version of the traditional Mexican Hat Dance tune. The record was promoted on *American Bandstand*, where the teens stood in a circle and did what was essentially the Mexican Hat Dance to the "new" rock 'n' roll record. Of virtually no musical or choreographic significance, "Mexican Hat Rock" and its accompanying dance are meaningful only as exemplars of the commercial exploitation of *American Bandstand*'s power to sell records. Because teens nationwide looked to the show to help them stay on top of the latest rock 'n' roll dance trends, any seemingly new dance demonstrated on the television program could prompt huge sales of even the most unoriginal of rock 'n' roll recordings.

In 1959, Dave Appell's combo came out with "Conga-Rock," to which the *Bandstand* kids lined up Conga fashion and did the basic 1-2-3-kick Conga step. The "new" rock 'n' roll record was essentially conga music with a rock 'n' roll beat. Appell also came out with a rock version of the Bunny Hop in the late '50s, which revived that dance craze for a short time.

As it wasn't just the teens who had money to spend in the 1950s and the record producers who had entrepreneurial impulses, hybrid rock 'n' roll dances were also invented by dance instructors eager to exploit adult ballroom dancers interested in maintaining currency with the latest cultural trends. In 1958, an article in the national trade publication *Dance Magazine* described the "Hula Rock," a new dance invented by Betty Mae Harris, a ballroom dance teacher and studio owner from Boone, Iowa. The dance combined basic ballroom dance figures, such as the box step, with movements from the popular rock 'n' roll dance the Stroll. The dance steps were to be done with swaying hip actions, reminiscent of the Hula."[44]

It is no coincidence that Harris's Hula-inspired rock 'n' roll–ballroom dance hybrid emerged when it did. During the late 1950s Americans were showing great interest not only in rock 'n' roll, but also in Hawaiian culture. In the wake of the democratic revolution that took place in Hawaii in 1954, an active campaign for statehood was underway among its residents. In 1958, even though the circling of a big hoop around one's hips had been done in cultures all over the world since ancient times, the Wham-O company made oodles of money selling a fad toy version of it called the "Hula Hoop." And on August 21, 1959, Hawaii officially became America's 50th state.

Prohibited Dances

While the ludicrously commercial, rock hybrid dances could be thought of as artistically offensive, there were other rock 'n' roll dances of the period that were considered socially offensive and an affront to good taste. One such dance was the Dog, which was strictly prohibited on *American Bandstand*. "Dick Clark wouldn't allow any dirty dancing," said Arlene Sullivan.[45] A sexually suggestive dance, the Dog requires the woman to turn around and bend over, angling her pelvis up in the air, as her partner dances up close behind her. The image is of two dogs engaged in sexual intercourse. Dancing too close together or doing any kind of grinding movements while slow dancing was also expressly forbidden on *Bandstand*.

Other Television Dance Shows

Though far more influential and much better known than any of the others, *American Bandstand* was not the only, nor was it the first, television program to feature dancing teens. It is *TV Teen Club*, hosted by the famed 1920s jazz bandleader Paul Whiteman, which is commonly considered the first teen television dance program. A Saturday evening dance and talent show to which Whiteman invited local teens, the ABC-TV network program was broadcast from Philadelphia and premiered in 1949 when, of course, teenagers were not yet dancing to rock 'n' roll.[46]

By the mid-1950s, however, scores of teen-oriented television dance programs driven by rock 'n' roll music sprung up in small and major cities all across the country.[47] Chicago had DJ Jim Lounsbury's *Bandstand Matinee*, which debuted in 1954 and aired weekdays from 4 to 5 P.M. Detroit had Dale Young's *Detroit Bandstand*, and New Haven had Jim Gallant's *Connecticut Bandstand*. St. Louis had the Saturday afternoon *St. Louis Hop*, while New York had *Studio Party*, hosted by Herb Sheldon, as well as *Teen Bandstand*, hosted by former Stork

Young teens dancing on *Hi-Jinx* in 1955. One of the many television teen dance programs, this Saturday night dance contest show was hosted by Al Jarvis and aired on KABC in Hollywood. (ABC/Photofest)

Club orchestra leader Ted Steele. In Los Angeles, there was *The Art Laboe Show,* and in Washington, D.C., the extremely popular *Milt Grant's Record Hop* (later re-titled *The Milt Grant Show*), which aired seven days a week at 5 P.M. Baltimore's *The Buddy Deane Show* was immortalized in the 1988 film *Hairspray,* which bitingly satirized the show's whites-only policy. The movie's fictional story revolved around efforts to racially integrate a TV teen-dance show, clearly modeled on Buddy Deane's popular program. Though produced and broadcast in different regions of the country, most of the teen-dance programs employed a format very similar to that of *American Bandstand.*[48]

Large cities often had programs that featured solely African-American teens, such as the Philadelphia area's *Mitch Thomas Show.* There were only a few television dance programs in the 1950s, however, that featured both black and white teens on the same show. And none of the programs ever allowed an integrated couple.[49]

One of the teen television dance programs of the era that was racially integrated from the get-go was the New York City–based show *The Big Beat,* hosted by Alan Freed. And the show would prove to be short-lived. Signed to host a 13-week television teen-dance series, which debuted July 12, 1957, on the ABC network, Freed was determined to combat the wild image of rock 'n' roll that had developed in association with many of his live music and dance events. Attempting to demonstrate that rock 'n' roll could be enjoyed by everyone in the family, he enlisted many white pop-oriented singers among the line-up of musical artists that appeared on his program. At the end of each show the teenagers in the audience would get up and dance to the music. It was during this dance segment, on the show's second episode, that one of the guest artists, the African-American singer Frankie Lymon, grabbed the hand of a white teenage girl from the audience and began to dance with her. Outrage ensued. The ABC network received such flack from its southern affiliates that the sponsors said they would discontinue their support of the show unless it would feature only white musical artists in the future. Freed refused to agree with this compromise and the show was discontinued after just two more episodes.[50]

As the decade was drawing to a close, the most revolutionary innovation that rock 'n' roll dancing would bring to the larger world of social dance was just beginning to boil. It would come in the form of a ridiculously simple dance that severed the defining element of partner dancing and forever changed the way couples danced "together." It was called the Twist. Why did it take the world by storm? What did it signify? And how was it to affect the future of rock 'n' roll dancing?

4

Twisting into 1960

"It's synthetic sex turned into a sick spectator sport," opined the Trinidad-born American dancer-choreographer Geoffrey Holder, in an *Ebony* magazine article he wrote about the Twist. "I deplore strongly what the Twist is doing to social dancing in America. As a dancer I am unmoved by it mainly because it is so static and downright dull and cheap."[1] Comedian Bob Hope likened the movements of the Twist to "a dog coming out of water."[2] Former President Dwight Eisenhower claimed, "I have no objection to the Twist, as such, but it does represent some kind of change in our standards. . . . What has happened to our concept of beauty and decency and morality?"[3]

Despite its detractors, the Twist has the distinction of being the biggest dance fad in the history of American popular music.[4] The Twist was also the first rock 'n' roll dance to be embraced by adults as well as by teens. Yet why, at the culmination of the 1950s, did so many Americans go wild over a ludicrously simple dance that involved nothing more than a rhythmic twisting motion of one's torso? "Both dances and contortions which pass for dances reveal something of the society that produces them, that makes a vogue of them," wrote Holder.[5] Tellingly, the Twist emerged and entranced the American population during a musically barren and emotionally disheartening period, a time when the rock 'n' roll music scene was desperately seeking a revitalizing influence, and America at large was in need of a reassuring boost of confidence.

By the late 1950s, the exciting and provocative "newness" of rock 'n' roll had begun to wane. Those who profited from the craze were finding it harder and harder to come up with fresh artists, sounds, songs, and dances that would grab the teens' interest, yet also meet with adult approval. It was the frantic attempts to keep producing catchy new rock 'n' roll records that resulted in many of those artistically pointless hybrid songs and dances. And because of television's increasingly important role in promoting the popularity of rock 'n' roll records, the visual and physical aspects of the singers became critical. Regardless of their musical abilities, in the late 1950s it was vital that up-and-coming rock 'n' roll performers look good on TV.[6]

So important was television becoming to American culture during the 1950s that even major political campaigns were seriously affected by its powerful influence. Early in the decade, Rosser Reeves of New York's Ted Bates advertising agency ushered in a revolutionary change in American political campaigning with his trendsetting television commercials in support of Eisenhower's bid for the presidency. The short campaign "spots" aired in October 1952 and featured the candidate in a one-shot, alone in the frame, answering questions posed by ordinary citizens. By the end of the decade, it was recognized that television had become an integral part of campaign politics when the televised debates between candidates John F. Kennedy and Richard M. Nixon proved a deciding factor in the 1960 presidential race.

Teen Idols

In an attempt to garner adult acceptance and a wider, mainstream audience for the music, Dick Clark had significantly sanitized rock 'n' roll with the kinds of performers, musical arrangements, and images of teenage fans he put forth on *American Bandstand*. Since the television program exerted such a strong influence on the record business, the aesthetics of Clark's show had come to dominate the rock 'n' roll music of the era. "The raw black music, which was seen as a threat by many adults, was out," said *American Bandstand* dancer Ray Smith, "because even in the late '50s, there was still plenty of racism. People would say unbelievable things like 'it's voodoo music that makes your kids jungle savages.'"[7]

The rock 'n' roll music of the late 1950s had taken on a calmer, more visually oriented sensibility and was more heavily influenced by polished pop sounds than by raw rhythm and blues. Its stars were no longer the wild, defiant types who had pioneered the new musical genre. Rather, they were clean-cut, handsome young artists (usually men) who sometimes, but not always, had musical talent. What they all had, however, was the ability to incite the swooning adoration of young teens. It was the era of the teen idol: a period of rock 'n' roll history that ran from 1958 to 1964, and that critics and hard-core rock 'n' roll enthusiasts characterize as a fallow time in terms of originality and musical excitement.

American Bandstand was the main platform for the introduction of the teen idols, most of whom became stars largely because of their frequent exposure on the television program. This batch of late '50s singing sensations has been referred to as "the Philadelphia phenomenon," as a disproportionate number of them hailed from Philadelphia or recorded on Philadelphia-based record labels.[8] Because they lived close by the studio, Philadelphia-area performers would often get invited to appear on *American Bandstand* when Clark had a last minute cancellation from a performing artist and needed a quick replacement.[9] Even a single appearance on the popular television show could turn an unknown singer into a household name.

Many of the teen idols were Italian Americans. For a lot of the first- and second-generation offspring of Italian immigrants, who populated the tough, working-class neighborhoods of South Philadelphia in the 1950s, to be a performing artist or a professional athlete was seen as a potential route to socio-economic advancement. The most popular of the Italian-American teen idols from Philadelphia were Frankie Avalon (Francis Thomas Avallone), Bobby Rydell (Robert Ridarelli), and Fabian (Fabiano Forte). Other well-known singing idols of the period included the Canadian Paul Anka, Jimmy Clanton from Louisiana, Freddy Cannon (Frederick Anthony Picariello) from Massachusetts, and Dion (Dion Francis DiMucci) and Bobby Darin (Walden Robert Cassotto) from New York. It has been suggested that Dick Clark intentionally sought out Italian-American singers so as to capitalize on the immense popularity of such crooners as Frank Sinatra and Perry Como, hoping that the public would carry over their association of Italians and singing talent from pop and opera into the rock 'n' roll arena.[10]

With their youthful good looks, the teen idols appealed directly to *American Bandstand*'s primary viewing audience, which according to a

Gallup poll was made up largely of high school freshmen and sophomores, and three times as many girls as boys. Over time, the show's audience had also grown to include many mothers of teenagers, who watched the program to learn about the music, dances, and fashions their youngsters preferred. Always the entrepreneur, Clark appealed directly to the mothers in his audience by issuing press releases boasting "Age No Barrier to *Bandstand* Beat." When he was on the air he would invite housewives to "roll up the ironing board and join us when you can."[11]

Adolescent girls were clearly mesmerized by the teen idols' romantic charms, and their mothers were undoubtedly comforted by the singers' boy-next-door qualities. Yet, despite their popularity and broad appeal, for the most part, the teen idols did not contribute significantly to the musical development of rock 'n' roll. By the end of the 1950s, it appeared that the rock 'n' roll revolution was a fad that was fizzling. In his textbook *Rock and Roll: Its History and Stylistic Development,* Joe Stuessy wrote that, by 1960, "much of the power of the first rock-and-roll shock wave had dissipated."[12]

As if to symbolically mark the culmination of that first tumultuous era of rock 'n' roll history, while fans were beginning to embrace a new, gentler style of performer, on March 24, 1958, Elvis Presley was drafted into the army. With Presley's induction into military service, rock 'n' roll seemed to have lost its prototypical performer, the artist most famously associated with the music's potential to shock and ignite controversy. It was around this same time that Little Richard turned away from rock 'n' roll to follow his fundamentalist religious beliefs, Jerry Lee Lewis was publicly ostracized for marrying his adolescent cousin, and Chuck Berry's popularity declined when he was arrested for violating the Mann Act, after allegedly having sex with a 14-year-old Apache waitress he had transported over state lines. Also, on February 3, 1959, three beloved 1950s rock 'n' roll performers were killed in a plane crash: Buddy Holly, Ritchie Valens, and J. P. "The Big Bopper" Richardson. Together on a rock 'n' roll concert tour through the Midwest, the three men were flying from a venue in Clear Lake, Iowa, to their next gig in Minnesota. Also on the tour was the singer Dion, who felt he could not afford to spend his money on air travel. Fortuitously, instead of getting onboard the fated flight, Dion chose to take the bus. In his song "American Pie," Don McLean called the date of the fatal crash "the day the music died."

While the music scene was adjusting to the pacifying changes in rock 'n' roll, the social-dance world was darkened by the dubious business methods of the big commercial dance-instruction studios. While most teens learned how to do the latest dances by copying their peers on *American Bandstand,* many adult social-dancers of the era flocked to professional dance studios, where they were taught ballroom dancing as well as some of the new rock 'n' roll dance trends. By the late 1950s, legal complaints were being lodged throughout the state of New York by patrons of instructional dance studios, who were claiming to have been swindled out of enormous amounts of money. One case involved a woman who agreed to pay $80 for four lessons and wound up in a series of contracts for which she had to pay more than $9,000. In another instance, a woman was forced to use $6,000 of her insurance savings to pay a dance studio bill, and a blind newsstand operator somehow found himself obligated for $11,000 worth of dance lessons. In 1958, New York state assemblyman Malcolm Wilson, of Yonkers, proposed a regulatory bill that would place strict controls on commercial dance studios, curbing the studios' apparently standard practice of utilizing high-pressure sales techniques.[13]

Prompted by complaints from hundreds of students—some claiming they had been induced to sign lifetime contracts "far in excess of their ability to pay"—a state-wide investigation was launched into the business practices of dance studios. The investigation revealed that some life-membership contracts required an upfront payment of more than $12,000. Three of the leading ballroom-dance franchises—the Dale Dance Studios, Fred Astaire, Inc., and the Arthur Murray Dance Studios—were accused of having violated lesson agreements.

In the aftermath of the investigation, the state's attorney general, Louis J. Lefkowitz, drew up a code of ethics for dance studios. All three of the major studios signed agreements to abide by the code, which required, among other things, that dance-lesson contracts be in writing, and include cancellation provisions.[14] In the early 1960s, similar legal initiatives in the state of California brought forth charges against the Fred Astaire and Arthur Murray chains, accusing them of fleecing customers through a "dancing-studio racket" that, as reported in the *New York Times,* has "probably reaped many millions of dollars from gullible persons throughout the country."[15] But it was not only the dance-teaching business that had its reputation tarnished in the 1950s. The decade was marked by disturbing congressional investigations and political events that upset Americans' faith in many aspects of their country and culture. Since the early years of the decade, Senator Joseph McCarthy had been scaring the country with accusations and hearings on Communist subversion in the government, Hollywood, and the military. Highly publicized hearings were also held in the '50s on organized crime activity and corruption in labor union leadership. By the end of the decade, Americans had grown fearful that disruptive forces and fraud were everywhere.

Contributing further to the nation's crisis of confidence, in 1957 the Russians scored a major victory in the space race with the launch of the first satellite, Sputnik. Such demonstration of technological achievement on the part of our Cold War enemy only exacerbated Americans' fears of Russia's nuclear weapons capabilities. And it was not long after the freedom fighter Fidel Castro took over the island of Cuba, on January 1, 1959, that it became clear to Americans that there was a Communist sympathizer governing a Soviet-allied country right off the shores of Florida.

Among the unsettling occurrences of the latter half of the decade, however, those most relevant to the world of rock 'n' roll music and dance were the scandalous goings-on in the television and radio industries. In 1955, the CBS television network scored a big hit with the blockbuster quiz show *The $64,000 Question*. In an attempt to emulate CBS's success, the NBC network debuted its own television quiz show, *Twenty-One,* which had as one of its winning contestants Charles Van Doren, son of Columbia University professor Mark Van Doren. In 1957, a former champion contestant, Herb Stempel, revealed that the show was rigged and confessed to having been forced to intentionally lose to Van Doren, whom the show's producers felt would be a more appealing "character" to the television viewers. Stempel's claims, which were proven to be true and also involved dishonesty on Van Doren's part, set off a huge scandal that called into question the integrity of all of the television quiz shows. Historian David Halberstam identifies this as a traumatic moment for the country, one that marked the "end of American innocence," as Van Doren had been a symbol of "the best America had to offer."[16]

Democratic congressional leaders were particularly interested in looking into any wrongdoings within the television industry, as it was suspected that, throughout the Fifties, members of the stations' regulatory body, the Federal Communications Commission (FCC), were being increasingly influenced by private enterprise. As Eisenhower's vice president, Richard Nixon, was now running for president, the Democrats sought to gain political advantage by emphasizing the degree of corruption that had been tolerated by the Eisenhower administration. They saw aggressive investigation of the television quiz shows as an opportunity to do so.[17] By 1959, most of the quiz programs had been taken off the air, their reputations ruined, as audiences felt they could no longer trust in the fairness of the competition.

In the radio industry, meanwhile, an even larger scandal was brewing. From the very beginning of rock 'n' roll music, manufacturers and distributors of rock 'n' roll recordings depended heavily on radio deejays for the promotion of their records. Frequent airplay on leading radio programs is what established a record's popularity and drove its sales. It became common practice, therefore, for record companies to give DJs significant sums of money or gifts in exchange for playing their records on the radio. This granting of what was often lavish compensation to the DJs was referred to as "payola." Countless DJs all across the country were receiving payoffs from record companies in many different fashions. Accused of being one of the primary recipients, Alan Freed took payola from a record distributing company in the form of checks made out to his wife's maiden name. Though never convicted of payola charges, Dick Clark was promoting singers on his television show who performed songs recorded by companies in which he had a financial interest. As soon as Congress started investigating payola charges, Clark relinquished all of his interests in music recording and publishing companies. Even if they had nothing to do with the creation of a song, DJs were sometimes offered shared songwriting credit on a rock 'n' roll record, as incentive to play it as often as possible on their radio shows. The more copies a record sold, the more money the song's "co-writer" would earn in royalties.

While it is easy to find ethical fault in the widespread practice of payola, it was largely out of other political and economic motivations that a variety of forces banded together to expose the practice and bring down the people and institutions involved. Despite extensive probing by the congressional investigative committee, the quiz show fixers had never been charged with breaking any actual laws. Eager to capitalize on the sentiments of many voters who were infuriated at being hoodwinked by the television industry with its rigged game shows, congressional leaders were happy to investigate payola charges, as the charges involved not only DJs, but players throughout the entire broadcasting industry.

The anti–rock 'n' roll music licensing organization ASCAP was also eager to play a role in exposing payola since it so directly involved rock 'n' roll DJs, as well as the producers of rock 'n' roll records, and the broadcasting outlets that played rock 'n' roll music. Still looking to bring down its competitor, BMI, which represented many rock 'n' roll songs, ASCAP saw the payola issue as a good opportunity to de-face the rock 'n' roll industry at large. On November 6, 1959, ASCAP presented a letter to the Congressional Subcommittee on Legislative Oversight charging bribery of DJs in the determination of what songs got radio airplay and what records the public was "surreptitiously in-duced to buy."[18] They alleged a conspiracy between DJs, broadcasters, and BMI to suppress genuine talent and to trick the public into buying mediocre records.

As Congress began its payola investigations, anti-rock 'n' rollers had a field day proclaiming how relieved they were to hear that DJs had to be paid to play such awful music,[19] and many DJs ultimately lost their jobs. Though proof of payola could cause a station to lose its FCC license and an individual could be charged with tax evasion if he or she did not report payola income, the practice itself had not been a federal crime. Only a few states had a criminal statute against it. How-ever, after much investigation and prolonged hearings, in September 1960, a federal bill was passed making payola a criminal offense.

Although the word "payola" is notoriously associated with the shameful bribery practices that permeated the radio and rock 'n' roll music industries of the late 1950s, the practice of paying for song pro-motion is firmly embedded in the history of American music. Lobby-ing to have one's song exposed to the public can be traced back to 1863 when the composer of "Tenting Tonight on the Old Camp Ground" gave the leader of the era's famous Hutchinson Singing Family a share of the song's royalties if the group would sing it at their enormously popular concerts. Around the turn of the 20th century, Tin Pan Alley composers commonly paid performers to sing their songs in a practice that was called "song plugging."

The word "payola" first appeared in print in the entertainment-industry trade publication *Variety* in 1916 when the Music Publishers' Protective Association was formed to curtail song plugging. The in-vention of the phonograph temporarily put an end to the practice, but it was quickly revived with the emergence of radio broadcasting in the 1920s. By the 1950s, the practice of payola was at an all-time high as the small, independent labels that produced many of the early rock 'n' roll recordings needed some way of combating the influence of the large record companies.[20] It could be argued that without payola, rock 'n' roll might never have evolved as successfully as it did.

Nevertheless, the payola scandal is often cited as a contributing factor to the dismal state of the rock 'n' roll scene at the end of the '50s and into the early '60s. As radio stations instituted measures to guard against future payola accusations, DJs were robbed of much of their freedom to choose which records to play. Many radio stations adopted Top 40 formats, in which the disc jockeys were required to play only the most popular hits, over and over again. This practice stifled the wide range of rock 'n' roll songs that had previously been heard over the airwaves. With each station now playing the same songs, dictated by mainstream tastes, rock 'n' roll music seemed to take on a monotonous homogeneity.[21] In addition, since the introduction of the teen idols, rock 'n' roll was losing its emphasis on driving dance rhythms. The words, vocal sounds, and physical attractiveness of the performers were becoming preeminent.[22] Nonetheless, young people were still eager to get out on the dance floor and move. And it may be mainly for this reason that a disillusioned America went crazy for a ridiculously rudimentary dance that reignited the population's enthusiasm for rock 'n' roll music and dancing.

The Twist

It was in the summer of 1960, the final year of the Fifties, that the Twist took off and ultimately catapulted to unprecedented popularity. It was danced all across the country to singer Chubby Checker's hit recording of "The Twist." In his comprehensive book on the phenomenon, *The Twist: The Story of the Song and Dance That Changed the World*, author Jim Dawson noted, "Chubby Checker's recording of 'The Twist' is the only non-holiday single ever to hit number one on the Hit Parade (in 1960), drop completely off the charts, and then, in a new burst of popularity, rise all the way to number one a second time (in 1962). . . . 'The Twist' occupied *Billboard*'s Top Forty for a combined thirty-three weeks, longer at the time than any other record except Bing Crosby's

'White Christmas.'"[23] However, the Twist did not begin with Chubby Checker's record, nor did it originate in 1960.

Like virtually all American vernacular dances, the Twist has its roots in African-American culture, and the form of the dance that became a national sensation is an altered version of the original movements. Released in 1959, the original recording of "The Twist" was by African-American rhythm and blues singer Hank Ballard and the Midnighters. Though Ballard is credited with having written the song, "The Twist" was actually a combination of modifications of two earlier songs. Ballard's recording became popular among black teens, who danced to it with torso-twisting motions.[24] According to Ballard, the actions of the dance were derived from spontaneous twisting movements that he had observed his musicians doing while they were playing their instruments. When Ballard's musicians twisted their torsos, they would also lift one of their legs up in the air. "It was dirty how they lifted their leg," Ballard has said. From these observations, Ballard got the idea to write a song about doing "the twist."[25]

It was when Ballard's group performed "The Twist" at a concert in Baltimore that the dance was first seen by the white teenagers, who sparked its explosion into a global craze. The white teens took the song to the city's popular TV teen dance program, *The Buddy Deane Show*, where they performed their own version of the dance. From there, the Twist spread to Philadelphia and was soon being done by the teens on Dick Clark's trend-setting *American Bandstand*.

There are two differing versions of the story of how the Twist initially came to Clark's attention. One version claims that Buddy Deane called Clark and told him about a new dance the kids were doing on his show to Ballard's "The Twist." He spoke of how innovative it was that the teens were dancing without touching their partners.[26] A raw-styled rhythm and blues singer who had a somewhat bawdy reputation and whose song lyrics were full of lewd double entendres, Ballard was not the kind of musical artist Clark would have welcomed on his show. Clark told Deane that he was not interested in Ballard's recording and described it as "a dirty record."[27] In another version of the story, which he relates in his memoir *Rock, Roll and Remember*, Clark claims that the Twist originally came to his attention when he saw a black couple doing it in the studio on *American Bandstand*. He described what they were doing as "a dance that consisted of revolving their hips in quick, half-circle jerks, so their pelvic regions were heaving in

Hank Ballard, the rhythm and blues singer credited with writing "The Twist." Ballard recorded the song in 1959, but it wasn't until Chubby Checker's cover version was released in 1960 that the song launched a dance craze that forever changed the way couples danced to rock 'n' roll music. (Photofest)

time to the music." Clark advised the cameramen to keep away from the black couple because, with its isolated pelvic actions, their dancing was "too suggestive" for his program. The white teenagers, however, were fascinated by the dance and started to imitate it.[28]

Because of how avidly the Philadelphia teens took to doing the Twist, Clark ultimately relented and allowed it to be danced on *American Bandstand*. However, he remained opposed to Ballard's record, which he deemed "too black."[29] Once committed to promoting the new dance on his show, Clark made it known to the owner of the Cameo-Parkway recording company that he wanted a cover version of Ballard's "The Twist" that he could use on *American Bandstand*. It was decided that the song would be recorded by a relatively unknown local African-American singer named Ernest Evans, whose youthful, upbeat, disarming persona was the opposite of Ballard's threatening edginess. It was supposedly Clark's wife (clearly thinking of Fats Domino) who came up with the idea of changing the mild-mannered, pudgy singer's name from Ernest Evans to Chubby Checker.[30]

Checker's specialty had been performing spot-on impressions of other vocal artists and his recording of "The Twist" was done as an exact mimicry of Ballard's rendition. Ballard recalls the first time he heard Checker's cover version of the song, it was playing on a pop radio station in Miami. Checker's imitation was so dead-on that for a moment Ballard was thrilled at the thought that his records might finally be breaking through to white markets, before he realized that what he was hearing was not his recording.[31] Checker's cover was released in July 1960 and prominently featured on *American Bandstand*. Suddenly, the Twist was all the rage among America's teens.

The Twist as "introduced" by Checker, however, did not involve any of the "naughty" leg lifting of Ballard's musicians. Checker danced it with both feet firmly planted on the floor, one slightly in front of the other, and with knees bent. In teaching TV audiences how to do

Chubby Checker performing the Twist, circa 1962. (Photofest)

the Twist, Checker advised, "just pretend you're wiping your bottom with a towel as you get out of the shower, and putting out a cigarette with both feet."[32] While lip-synching to his record, Checker also added some jerky movements of the arms, generally keeping them waist-level and moving in opposition to one another, yet occasionally lifting one arm overhead and gesturing as if twirling a lasso.[33] But according to *American Bandstand* dancer Ray Smith, Checker only did those big arm movements because he was a performer and was trying to make the dance more visually entertaining to watch. "When we danced the Twist, it was just the hips moving," said Smith.[34]

When the Philadelphia teenagers first starting doing the Twist, before the broad acceptance it eventually garnered, the dance was considered sexually daring and was frowned upon by adults. At record hops at the Catholic schools, Smith remembers teenagers dancing it while surrounded by a circle of onlookers who would serve to block the dancers from view. As soon as the chaperones realized what was going on, they would break up the circle and reprimand the kids they had caught "Twisting."[35]

Deejay Jerry Blavat recalls playing the Hank Ballard version of "The Twist" at a dance he ran at the Dixon House in South Philadelphia in the late 1950s. "It was the summer, so the kids were dancing outside," he said. "The neighbors across the street would sit out and watch them and when they saw the kids doing the Twist they complained to Dixon House. They said the kids were doing a lewd, dirty dance, 'shaking their asses.' I had to go from house to house explaining to all the neighborhood residents that the Twist was not something dirty; it was just a dance."[36]

Just as Dick Clark did much to sanitize rock 'n' roll in general, Chubby Checker played a tremendous role in cleaning up the Twist, which is surely what allowed it to achieve such widespread popularity. Checker has admitted that the Twist involved "moving the hips and that was nasty" in 1960. But with his warm, teddy-bear image when he did the Twist, Checker explained, "it wasn't nasty."[37]

There are no actual steps to the Twist. The dance consists simply of standing in one spot and rotating at the waist in time to the beat of the music. Yet despite, or perhaps because of, the monotony of its one and only motion, individuals evolved different styles and variations to distinguish their personal way of Twisting. According to Checker, you didn't have to be a great dancer to do the Twist; all that was needed was a little imagination. "That was the success of it," he has opined.[38] Nevertheless, once the dance became a fad, the Arthur Murray studios advertised Twist instruction in "6 Easy Lessons for $25."[39]

Although Ballard indisputably inaugurated the Twist dance fad, dance historians Marshall and Jean Stearns, in their book *Jazz Dance: The Story of American Vernacular Dance,* point out the existence of earlier forms of twisting dances. According to the Stearns, "the swaying motion of the Twist was employed long ago in Africa and by the Negro folk in the South . . . blues shouters of the twenties used it as they raised their arms to belt out a tune; and in the thirties it was inserted during the breakaway (where partners separated) of the Lindy."[40] Around the turn of the 20th century, the legendary African-American entertainer Bert Williams performed a dance dubbed the Williams Mooche, or Grind, which the Stearns describe as "employing movements similar to the Twist . . . [and having] a subtle flow that would have made our rock-and-roll devotees look like mechanized monkeys."[41] In 1912, the lyrics of a popular song of the day, "Messin' Around," instructed dancers to "stand in one spot, nice and light, twist around with all your might."[42] The 1913 song "Ballin' the Jack," which inspired a wildly popular dance craze, included similar lyrics, instructing dancers to "twis' around and twis' around with all your might." Those lyrics, however, were interpreted, not as the back-and-forth, washing machine-like rotating motion of the Twist, but rather as a sequence of movements in which the protruding pelvis is rotated around in a circle, usually with a bounce on each beat.[43] Yet it is highly likely that Americans, particularly in African-American communities, had been "twisting" on the dance floor for many years prior to 1960. Dating all the way back to the 1840s (with the "Grape Vine Twist"), and particularly since the 1920s, many popular songs can be found that feature the word "twist" in their title or lyrics.[44]

Unlike the other rock 'n' roll dances of the 1950s, which were symbolic badges of the era's youth culture, the Twist underwent an amazing "cross-over" into the adult population. Though the dance's popularity receded among teens at the end of 1960, the lull in the excitement was simply a reprieve. The dance was soon to morph into an extraordinary phenomenon that was enthusiastically embraced by Americans of all ages, races, and classes. The astounding resurgence in the Twist's popularity was launched in the fall of 1961, in the most unlikely of places.

The Peppermint Lounge on West 45th Street in Manhattan, the New York nightclub where celebrities and working-class toughs gathered to dance the Twist, circa 1961. (© Bettmann/CORBIS)

It happened at the Peppermint Lounge, a dingy rock 'n' roll bar on West 45th Street in New York City. Needing to spark business, the Lounge's publicist arranged for celebrities and members of society to visit the club, where they rubbed shoulders with its regular clientele of working-class toughs and danced to the Twist tunes played by the house band, a group from New Jersey known as Joey Dee and the Starliters. The presence of the celebrities attracted the *New York Journal-American's* society columnist Igor Cassini, a.k.a. Cholly Knickerbocker. After watching a Russian-born aristocrat dance the Twist at the club one night, Knickerbocker wrote in his "Smart Set" column, "The Twist is the new teenage dance craze. But you don't have to be a teenager to do the Twist." Reports on dancing the Twist at the Peppermint Lounge soon followed in other newspapers and magazines and within just a short time noted names from the theater world—the club was located in Manhattan's theater district—began stopping in to see what all the excitement was about. Truman Capote, Marilyn Monroe, Tallulah Bankhead, Shelley Winters, and Judy Garland started dropping in to dance the Twist.[45] The Peppermint Lounge very quickly became "the" place to go and the club's usual clientele was enmeshed with high-society types, show business celebrities, and prominent political-figures. The atmosphere at the Peppermint Lounge was described as the Rolls Royce set beginning to mingle with the Motorcycle set.[46]

The *New York Times* reported, "Café society has not gone slumming with such energy since its forays into Harlem in the Twenties. Greta Garbo, Noel Coward, Elsa Maxwell, Tennessee Williams, the Duke of Bedford and Countess Bernadotte—often in black tie or Dior gown—vie with sailors, leather-jacketed drifters and girls in toreador pants for admission to the Peppermint's garish interior . . . the lure is a tiny dance floor undulating with the Twist."[47] Eventually a professional choreographer was brought in to stage a show by "The Peppermint Twisters," an ensemble of stage dancers who performed the Twist so fast that it was said that the fringe on their costumes moved at a speed of 80 miles an hour.[48]

A Peppermint West franchise was opened in Hollywood, and clubs, restaurants, and dance halls all over the country rushed to provide places for people to congregate and dance the Twist. A nationwide Twist mania ensued. On television, Dick Van Dyke and Mary Tyler Moore, as well as Fred and Wilma Flintstone, were seen doing the Twist, while the news programs broadcast fuzzy images of Mercury astronauts Twisting in zero gravity. In a scene from the Broadway play *Come Blow Your Horn*, when he normally danced the Cha-Cha, actor Hal March did the Twist instead. And in a performance for an audience of airmen at advanced-warning radar bases in the Arctic Circle, Bob Hope quipped: "A guy froze to death doing the Twist; they couldn't bury him, they had to screw him in the ground."[49] It was even reported that the President and Jackie Kennedy, along with the First Lady's sister Princess Lee Radziwill, were spotted Twisting at a black-tie party in the Blue Room of the White House.[50] The 1962 Broadway musical *Mr. President*, choreographed by Peter Gennaro, featured a lively White House party scene in which the guests danced "The Washington Twist."

It was not just adults whom the Twist attracted to the rock 'n' roll dance floor, but children, too. This author remembers, as a three-year-old, attending a birthday party for the little girl who lived next door, in the very early 1960s. Along with the typical "Pin the Tail on the Don-key"–type games, the party festivities also included a Twist contest for the tots. (The author won first prize.)

By the early 1960s, the Twist had become an unofficial "brand," with every form of business imaginable trying to capitalize on the dance's widespread popularity. One could purchase Twist Barbie dolls, hats, shoes, boots, dresses, slacks, garters, cuff links, sweaters, and girdles, and even acquire a Twist hairdo, along with specific Twist hair products, as well as a corkscrew-shaped Twist chair, or a spaghetti line called the Twist developed by a Brooklyn pasta company.[51] The record industry went crazy producing Twist-inspired singles, such as Chubby Checker's "Let's Twist Again" and "Slow Twistin'," along with Joey Dee and the Starliters' "Peppermint Twist," Gary "U.S." Bonds's "Dear Lady Twist," Bobby Rydell's "Teach Me to Twist," Sam Cooke's "Twistin' the Night Away," Wilbert Harrison's "Kansas City Twist," The Champs' "Tequila Twist," Jimmy Clanton's "Twist On Little Girl," Billy Haley & His Comets' "Florida Twist" and "The Spanish Twist," and the Chipmunks' "The Alvin Twist," plus countless more, as well as multitudinous long-playing albums of Twist songs.

Hollywood followed suit with the rapid production of four low-budget films with Twist in the title: *Twist Around the Clock* (1961) and *Don't Knock the Twist* (1962), both starring Chubby Checker and produced by Sam Katzman (who had made *Rock Around the Clock* and *Don't Knock the Rock*); *Hey, Let's Twist* (1961); and *Twist All Night* (1961), starring Louis Prima. All were critical bombs, though film buffs find *Hey, Let's Twist* of note in that it represents the screen debut of actor Joe Pesci, who was a guitarist with the Starliters at the time and appears as an extra in the film.

Despite its confounding popularity, the Twist also had its critics. Lou Brecker, the owner of New York's famous ballroom dance establishment, Roseland, said of the Twist: "It is lacking in true grace, and since we have previously outlawed rock and roll as a feature at Roseland, we likewise will not permit the Twist to be danced."[52] In November 1961, an orthopedic surgeon reported to the *Medical Tribune* that he was seeing more and more knee injuries—the kind usually sustained while playing football—among Twisting teenagers. He explained that the injuries were caused by vigorous rotation of the knee, the ligaments of which are not designed to handle such lateral movement. When excessive strain is put on knee ligaments, the person usually stops doing whatever is causing the pain, but in the case of the Twist, the surgeon opined that teenagers seem to be so hypnotized by

Performers dancing the Twist in the 1961 film *Hey, Let's Twist*. Considered a bomb, the movie is noteworthy only because actor Joe Pesci makes his screen debut as a guitarist with Joey Dee and the Starliters, the house band that played the Twist music at the Peppermint Lounge. (Paramount Pictures/Photofest)

the music and rhythm that they are not aware of the strain. The Society of New Jersey Chiropractors came out with a public statement against the Twist, branding it "a potentially hazardous torque movement causing strains in the lumbar and sacroiliac areas." A Chicago physician reported treating three back injuries in patients he deemed old enough to know better than to do the Twist.[53]

The most significant aspect of the Twist, however, has nothing to do with its physical twisting actions, nor its extraordinary popularity. Its real import lies in how definitively it broke up the dancing couple. A couple doing the Twist together actually danced completely independently from one another. Unlike the Jitterbugging that had been the mainstay of earlier rock 'n' roll dancing, the Twist was done without making physical contact. Partners positioned themselves just casually facing each other, their relationship evoking a cool, impersonal tone. Displaying no outward concern for what one's partner was doing, the Twister was utterly absorbed in his or her personal involvement with the music and the experience of moving to it.

By granting social dancers the permission to move independently, the Twist boldly defied dance-floor conventions. It was perhaps for this reason, its celebration of the individual, a notion that lies at the heart of American ideology, that this silly dance was so zealously embraced. At a time when Americans had become doubtful, distrustful, and disappointed by so many aspects of their culture, the Twist provided the opportunity to celebrate a very American ideal, the practice of individual freedom.

In his 1972 book *The Story of Rock,* author Carl Belz suggests that the independent-yet-together nature of the Twist could be viewed as a visual reflection of how rock 'n' roll music had always been experienced by its teenage fans. Fifties teens had listened to rock 'n' roll on personal-sized transistor radios or with a mass audience that was sharing the same experience but feeling it individually. The bond among the teenage dancers was in the music they were hearing, but their physical separation from one another showed that that bond was privately felt.[54]

Unlike artistic forms of dance, which can be individual platforms for personal expression, social dance forms are always reflections of the larger society. As such, the pre-Twist rock 'n' dancing practiced by the Fifties teens served, in part, to reinforce the era's conventional norms of social behavior, dress, and gender roles. When attending a dance event, it was important to be appropriately attired and to exhibit proper manners when asking or being asked to dance. Since most of the rock 'n' roll dances of the period were still partner dances, boys were expected to politely approach a girl and invite her to join him on the dance floor. Not only would he initiate the invitation, but throughout the dance he would select and lead her through specific moves, and afterwards escort her back to where she had been sitting—all by way of echoing the traditional male roles of leader, thinker, and protector.[55]

While the rock 'n' roll dancing of the 1950s represented changing social attitudes, for many years it also continued to reflect elements of the conformist and conservative values of the decade. For example, while teens may have started dancing "alone," they were usually all engaged in performing the same basic dance movements. Though they may have been imbuing the movements with their own individual styles, all of the dancers on the floor at any given time would be doing the Twist, or some other commonly designated dance. And also, while it was widely accepted for girls to dance with girls at record hops or parties, one would not have seen two boys dancing together in public. "Boys never danced with boys—absolutely never," said Al Decker, who was a teenager living in the Midwest during the 1950s.[56] Such an act would have carried a sexual connotation that the conservatism of the times would not have permitted.

Although the teens may have observed many of the conventions of social dancing they had been taught by adults, when the young '50s rebels began to dance to rock 'n' roll music, even before the Twist, they were already starting to change some of the old social rules. During the Swing era, one sometimes saw women Jitterbugging with other women at family gatherings or at parties, as the carefree movements of the dance could easily be performed with gender-neutral partnering. Yet the Swing-era women typically danced with each other only when their husbands or dates did not want to dance, or when they were out together with a group of women and did not have access to a male partner. It was during the early rock 'n' roll era that it became increasingly more common to see girls Jitterbugging with girls in complete defiance of adult social conventions. Unwilling to wait to be asked to dance by a boy, or not wanting to dance with a boy at all, girls would go out onto the dance floor with one another and Jitterbug together, perhaps taking turns playing the roles of leader and follower.[57] Rock 'n' roll music provided such a powerful impetus to move that the girls' desire to dance trumped any respect they might have had for social-dance rules.

By the end of the 1950s, rock 'n' roll dancing no longer prioritized the traditional male-female couple, but rather the individual. When the independent dancing came in, said one Fifties teen, "the social contact was lost, it was more like show time."[58] The sight of individuals out on a dance floor Twisting freely and separately from each other in improvised actions of their own invention flew in the face of so many social conventions, which were soon to be challenged within society at large. With no leader or follower or partner-work rules, traditional gender roles became utterly meaningless. The rise of individualized dancing that began with the choreographed group dances and took off with the Twist foreshadowed not only the rise of feminism, but also the values of the "Me Generation" of the 1970s. When dancing independently with a partner women were suddenly equal to men, and the most important goal was for each person to create and perform his or her own movements.

Moving On

As the 1950s drew to a close, the focus of the rock 'n' roll music and dance industry was on the commercially driven goal of coming up with the next "Twist," a new dance fad that would emulate the Twist's remarkable simplicity and broad appeal. Tellingly, though the Twist did not become passé among the general population until the summer of 1963, it was not long after the adults began Twisting in 1961 that American teenagers rejected the dance. It was no longer "their" dance and if their parents were doing it, it could no longer represent any kind of rebellion. Fearful of losing out on teen dollars, record producers worked furiously to come up with new dances that the teenagers could adopt as their own. It is undoubtedly for this reason that the first few years of the 1960s featured the invention of a mind-boggling parade of new dances, which were performed like the Twist, positioned across from yet moving independently from one's partner. Also like the Twist, the dances typically consisted of one basic body action or gesture that was a pantomimic, "charades"-like representation of the words of the song. The litany of these early '60s dances included the Mashed Potato, Monkey, Frug, Hitch-Hike, Fly, Hully Gully, Watusi, Swim, Jerk, Elephant Walk, Loco-Motion, and dozens of others.

Yet it was not just the influence of the Twist that makes the rock 'n' roll dance floor of the early Sixties feel very much like that of the late '50s. Many American historians mark the end of the 1950s in the Sixties, usually at the end of 1963. The cultural trends and essential spirit of the 1950s are commonly considered to have ended with the assassination of President John F. Kennedy on November 22, 1963. The years that followed Kennedy's death were decidedly different from those that preceded it in ways too numerous and profound to contemplate in these pages, while the years before his death in many ways reflect a continuation of the attitudes that drove and characterized the previous decade.

The history of rock 'n' roll and the dancing it provoked can be drawn along a similar timeline. The end of the Fifties era in rock 'n' roll music is generally marked by the beginning of the "British invasion," a revivifying new movement launched by the arrival in the United States of the Beatles. The revolutionary new rock 'n' roll group from England took America by storm with their appearance on *The Ed Sullivan*

Show on February 9, 1964—just 11 weeks after JFK was shot. The Beatles were seen by an estimated 73 million viewers, the largest audience, by far, in the history of television.[59] America's fading rock 'n' roll scene was injected with Beatlemania, a fresh force that would set it on a whole new evolutionary path, both musically and dance-wise—or, more accurately, non-dance-wise.

By 1964, not only were teens no longer Jitterbugging to the latest rock tunes, but they had long since discarded the idea of partner dancing, and even the Twist was a relic of the past. A significant amount of the rock 'n' roll music written in the 1960s was designed for listening rather than dancing, much like the cerebral jazz music that had preceded the birth of rock 'n' roll. In the liner notes for the first album recorded by the trendy Sixties folk trio Peter, Paul, and Mary, in 1962, instructions are given as to how to listen to the record: "It [the music] deserves your exclusive attention. No dancing, please."[60] Clearly, the pendulum had swung. But that's the beginning of another story.

5

Fifties Nostalgia

By the end of the 1960s, the United States was in a state of discord. Americans were struggling to come to terms with such divisive issues as the war in Vietnam, the assassination of Martin Luther King, hippies, and rampant drug use. Tensions continued to mount over the next few years with the Kent State shootings, Watergate, and the oil crisis. It is not surprising, therefore, that in the early 1970s the American population, surely desirous of an escape from present conditions, got swept up in a surge of Fifties nostalgia. Worn down by the rending issues of the day, Americans rushed to devour the music, dancing, spirit, and fashions of the 1950s, seemingly ravenous for a coming together, a re-affirmation of traditional values, and a return to a time when all was well in America—or at least a time when all appeared to be well.

According to historian David Halberstam, it was the falsely harmonious portrayal of the Fifties featured in the era's television programs for which Americans of the 1970s grew nostalgic.[1] In reality, the cultural tensions that exploded in the Sixties had been brewing throughout the 1950s. Nonetheless, warm feelings and an ardent longing for the 1950s emerged with a vengeance at the beginning of the Seventies as the country conjured fond remembrances of the era through recreations of the period's fun music and dancing, the sporting of Fifties clothing fashions, and the adoption of the "greaser" (see below) as the iconic image of the period. While the professional entertainment industry produced '50s-themed concerts, stage shows, movies, and television programs, schools, recreational centers, and community groups all over the country were hosting proms, dances, performances, and gym nights based on the rock 'n' roll music, dances, attitudes, and symbols of the bygone era. While it was the general political and cultural climate of the early 1970s that provided the perfect fuel for this escapist trip down memory lane, the '50s nostalgia trend was directly instigated by a rock 'n' roll revival movement, which was ushered in by a musical group that came to be known as Sha-Na-Na.

Rock 'n' Roll Revival

The notion of revisiting the early rock 'n' roll music of the 1950s was not an idea born of the early '70s. Fifties musical nostalgia had actually been going on since the late 1950s, the period when the style of rock 'n' roll music had changed dramatically and taken on a more mainstream passivity and homogeneity. It was at that time—after endless requests from listeners to play the old rock 'n' roll songs which had launched the genre in the mid-'50s—that Hollywood-based deejay Art Laboe started to air a show entirely devoted to these older recordings. He coined the term "oldies but goodies" to describe the old records. He then issued a compilation album of the old songs, which he titled "Oldies But Goodies in Hi-Fi." The recording entered *Billboard's* chart of best-selling albums on September 21, 1959, and remained there for three years. In the album's liner notes, Laboe opined that those early rock 'n' roll songs had a Proustian power to bring back past memories.[2] The playing of oldies quickly became, and has remained, a popular component of radio rock music programming. So by the time the rock 'n' roll revival movement took off in the early '70s, it was already known how potent a nostalgic tool '50s rock 'n' roll music could be.

The original rock 'n' roll revival group of the '70s was formed at Columbia University in 1969 when The Kingsmen, the college's male *a capella* group, began adding '50s doo-wop songs to their repertoire. They soon became a campus craze and ultimately changed their name to Sha-Na-Na. The name derives from chanted syllables in the chorus of the 1958 hit song "Get a Job," by the Silhouettes.[3] The group's fame skyrocketed after they performed at the watershed Woodstock rock music festival in August 1969 and then appeared in the 1970 film documenting the festival. Sha-Na-Na also made an appearance in the blockbuster

'50s nostalgia film *Grease* (see below), and starred in their own hit television show, a syndicated program that aired from 1977 to 1982.

Sha-Na-Na's initial success can be largely credited to the promotional efforts of Neil Bogart of Casablanca Records. "To build this group," Bogart has said, "we created a music industry trend. We called it rock 'n' roll revival. With slogans, stickers, buttons, and industry and consumer contests, and even black leather jackets for our promotion staff, we brought back the fifties."[4]

In their highly entertaining, intricately choreographed shows, the group performed the old hit songs with an abundance of energy and an air of affectionate satire. Designed more to entertain than to reflect the authentic rock 'n' roll dancing of the era, the group's choreography has been described as "callisthenic," and performed "with the precision of the Rockettes."[5] A *New York Times* critic opined that Sha-Na-Na's "massive choreography makes each number a virtual Busby Berkeley routine" and that they "leap around the stage, from microphone to microphone, posing, and doing unison dance steps."[6] Group members were also known to imitate the movements of the original musical artists, giving their renditions of Chuck Berry's famous duck walk or

Sha-Na-Na, the fun-loving group that started the '50s rock 'n' roll revival movement of the early 1970s. (Photofest)

scrambling all over the piano keys à la Jerry Lee Lewis.[7] But while they imitated their movements, the group members did not costume themselves like the original artists. Sporting slicked-back hair, white socks, and cigarette packs rolled in their T-shirt sleeves, they dressed, instead, as "greasers," the delinquent juveniles, or "hoods," whom the media liked to portray as the fans of early rock 'n' roll.[8]

Menacing gangs of rock 'n' roll-loving, motorcycle-riding or hot rod car-racing hoodlums, "greasers" were a working-class youth sub-culture that emerged in the 1950s, contributing considerably to rock 'n' roll's ignoble reputation. While their greatest enthusiasm was for trou-blemaking, so strong was their affiliation with rock 'n' roll music—usually of the rockabilly type—that the U.K.'s equivalent of greaser gangs in the 1960s were called rockers. The greasers' primary identify-ing characteristic, however, was the pomade, or other kinds of greasy gels and creams, they used to fashion their hair. They would style their hair slicked back, built up high into a pompadour, or with the sides combed to the back and then impolitely parted in a manner that was considered to resemble a duck's behind and was called a "duck-tail," "duck's ass" or "DA." Greaser attire usually consisted of jeans, a black or white T-shirt with rolled-up sleeves (in which a pack of ciga-rettes could be stashed), a leather jacket, and motorcycle boots.

As these toughs were seen to represent teen rebellion at its most extreme, their hairdos and clothing styles were undoubtedly adopted by teenage boys who wanted to be perceived as "cool." Fictionalized images of greasers were typically portrayed as urban ethnic types or rural Southerners, such as those in the 1953 Hollywood film *The Wild One*. Yet while the "greaser" look and persona, as recreated in nostalgic movies and television programs of later years, has become the signa-ture image of the defiant young '50s rock 'n' roll fan, it is unlikely that most boys who listened and danced to rock 'n' roll in the '50s actu-ally dressed or acted like greasers.

Inadvertently, though perhaps tellingly, with Sha-Na-Na's revivi-fication of '50s rock 'n' roll music, the rock 'n' roll dance floor once again served as a platform for the display of racial issues. In 1983 Sha-Na-Na performed a concert in the South African territory of Bo-phuthatswana (then an independent province). During the concert, the musicians invited audience members to come up onstage and dance with them. Denny Greene, who was the group's sole black musi-cian, was the only performer who could not find a partner who would agree to dance with him onstage. He extended invitations to four different white women, each of whom refused him. In a rage, he stormed offstage. When audience members yelled out, "Where's Greene?" Sha-Na-Na member Jon "Bowzer" Bauman told them Greene would come back if someone would dance with him. Bauman was successful in recruiting a volunteer who agreed to dance with Greene. However, Greene did not return to the stage and was quoted the next day in a South African newspaper alleging racism. Subsequently, an executive from the concert venue, the Sun City Superbowl, refuted Greene's claims of racism by explaining that the reason Greene could not readily find a dance partner was because South African people are too shy to join in that kind of audience participation.[9]

Despite their enormous popularity, Sha-Na-Na did have its detractors and they came from two opposing camps. Because the group brought both homage and fun to their renditions of the music they were criticized by early rock 'n' roll fans for spoofing such "important" music and by sophisticated rock fans for devoting their efforts to the performance of such simplistic, silly songs.[10] Nonetheless, Sha-Na-Na's influence on the '70s generation was tremendous. Not only did they motivate young people to want to go back and hear the original recordings of the music they performed, but they also inspired many teens to want to play that sort of rock 'n' roll music themselves.

"The real attraction to Fifties music for me in the Seventies came through Sha-Na-Na—we were just trying to do them. The fact that the songs are basically three and four chords didn't hurt either—a bad guitar player like myself could play them well," explained Craig Evans, who was typical of many teenagers drawn to the performance of early rock 'n' roll music during the '70s nostalgia craze. Evans formed a Fifties "garage band" when he was in junior high and continued it through his high school and college years. Like Sha-Na-Na, Evans's group exuded both a respect for the music and a sense of humor about the performance of it. "One of the teachers named us the Eggsuckers as a joke and we kept it," explained Evans. "At college we were called Waldo and the Geeks—Geeks being the term for non-Greeks, although most of us were frat guys. The name is sort of like the Eggsuckers in that regard."[11]

While Sha-Na-Na is generally considered the catalyst for the nostalgia trend that blasted off in the early '70s, one of the group's original members, vocalist Richard Joffee, argued that the group's popularity could not be attributed to nostalgia alone. A large percentage of the group's fans were teenagers who would have been too young to even remember the 1950s. Joffee claimed that those teens' interest in embracing the '50s rock 'n' roll revival movement was their generation's way of acknowledging that the changes they had been working for throughout the Sixties had occurred. Now that they felt they had put their stamp on American culture, it was okay for them to look back and embrace history. "In short," Joffee wrote in a 1973 article in *The Village Voice*, "the pervasive feeling that sparked the revival was a two-sided attitude toward the '50s. We could now enjoy the past because we had succeeded in transcending it." Joffee characterized the nostalgia craze as a ritual by which the current youth culture reaffirmed itself by assimilating the past. "In the nation at large the feeling of community has vanished," he wrote. "There is a void crying to be filled." Rock is establishing that sense of community by welcoming in *all* of it, he opined, and creating a sense of continuity by acknowledging rock's roots.[12]

Fifties Nostalgia on Stage and Screen

Yet, while the pop music scene was beginning to enjoy a revival of Fifties rock 'n' roll, it was the hit 1972 Broadway musical *Grease* that reinforced that trend and ignited the Fifties nostalgia movement among the general population. An affectionate spoof of '50s teens, *Grease* is set in 1959 and features '50s-style rock 'n' roll music and dancing, yet its theme of high school life explores timeless issues to which virtually all audiences can relate. An enormous hit, playing 3,388 performances before it closed in 1980, *Grease* became Broadway's longest-running show. (It held that distinction until 1983, when *A Chorus Line* beat its record.) "*Grease* appeared at the right time. Had it opened in the late '60s, it would have been politically tear-gassed and given those two fatal labels: irrelevant and escapist," opined a critic for New York's *Daily News*.[13] In 1978, a film version of *Grease* was released, starring John Travolta. A blockbuster hit, it remains one of the most commercially successful movie musicals ever made. According to a film critic writing in *The Village Voice*, "The dances (mainly mass shimmy-twists or parodies of old doo-wop acts) are the best things in the movie."[14]

The cast of the 1972 Broadway musical *Grease*, an affectionate look back at the music, dancing, and teenage culture of the 1950s. (Photofest)

But while *Grease* was not its first Fifties rock 'n' roll musical, Broadway had been notably slower to embrace the rock 'n' roll craze than Hollywood had been. While rock 'n' roll movies had been produced by the dozens since the mid-1950s, it wasn't until 1960 that the first rock 'n' roll stage musical, *Bye Bye Birdie*, opened on Broadway. An upbeat satire of the impact of rock 'n' roll on the American public, *Bye Bye Birdie* was about a soon-to-be-inducted-into-the-army rock 'n' roll star, clearly modeled on Elvis Presley. "In its celebration of fifties America, the musical was slyly nostalgic for an innocence already lost. It deftly appealed to and mocked American credulity," wrote drama critic John Lahr.[15]

Yet, despite its historical significance as the first rock 'n' roll musical, unlike *Grease*, which is driven by a score of '50s-style rock 'n' roll tunes, *Bye Bye Birdie* really contains only two rock songs, performed as parodies, with lots of Elvis-like gyrating. And even though the show

John Travolta, as a Fifties teen, dancing with Annette Charles (as actress Eve Arden looks on) in the 1978 blockbuster film musical *Grease*. (Paramount Pictures/Photofest)

contained a wealth of acclaimed choreography, the dancing consisted mainly of theatre-dance routines featuring the show's leading lady, actor-dancer Chita Rivera, and vaudevillian antics by the musical's other adult star, song-and-dance man Dick Van Dyke.

Though the show was originally conceived in 1958, it took two years of re-writes and much persuasion by the show's producer Edward Padula before *Bye Bye Birdie*'s director-choreographer Gower Champion could be convinced to take on the job. Champion and his wife, Marge, were well known as an adagio dance team, performing in nightclubs, movies, and on television. Yet, Champion loathed rock 'n' roll. He viewed it as a fad and had always refused to incorporate it into the couple's dance act. It was because he felt the original version of *Bye Bye Birdie* was nothing more than a straight satire on a rock 'n' roll singer that Champion initially turned down the invitation to direct and choreograph the show. "I wanted social commentary," he said, "with the emphasis not on the singer but on how and why masses of people reacted to him."[16] And it was exactly this concept that the one

Dick Gautier playing Conrad Birdie (a take-off on Elvis Presley) surrounded by adoring fans in 1960's *Bye Bye Birdie*, the first Broadway musical to revisit the early years of rock 'n' roll. (Photofest)

rock 'n' roll number in the show that contains choreography conveys. As Conrad Birdie, the Elvis-inspired character, sings "Honestly Sincere," his pulsating body movements generate a delirium among the teens and townsfolk that results in a mass collapse of everyone onstage. Champion has said that he originally tried to stage this number with formal dance patterns, but ultimately realized it was stifling the fun of it. "The scene needed a wild, improvisational quality and I think I finally achieved it with twisting, falling bodies fixed in position. The only person who moves around a lot is Birdie."[17]

The popular 1963 film version of *Bye Bye Birdie*, starring Ann-Margret and choreographed by Onna White, featured little more in the way of '50s rock 'n' roll dancing than did the Broadway show. While one can catch quick glimpses of Jitterbugging couples in the "Honestly Sincere" scene, the big teen ensemble dance sequence, "Lotta' Livin' To Do," is essentially a Swing-flavored show dance number with Cha-Cha steps, Jive footwork, and Bob Fosse-inspired movements dominating the choreographic vocabulary.

While the Hollywood rock 'n' roll films of the 1950s theatricalized the depiction of the era's rock 'n' roll dancing through choreography that drew upon the advanced skills of professional Swing dancers, the Broadway rock 'n' roll musicals (and the films subsequently based on them) theatricalized the period dancing largely through the incorporation of theater-dance vocabulary and a Broadway-jazz performance style. While the raucous dance numbers in *Grease*, choreographed by Patricia Birch, were certainly modeled on the actual social dances of the period (most notably the invigorating "Hand Jive" sequence), the choreography also incorporates familiar show-dance steps. While the utilization of theatrical dance steps and styles compromises the choreography's period authenticity, it does not seem to detract as much from the productions' depictions of Fifties' youth as did the use of professional Swing dancers and their competitive maneuvers in the rock 'n' roll films made in the 1950s. Many of the show-dance steps that the Broadway choreographers combined with Fifties rock 'n' roll moves had a juvenile quality to them that worked to further the development of the teenagers' young, fresh characters. As long as the dancing feels true to the characters performing it, audiences are likely to accept it as "real." While they may seem truer to reality, the nostalgic stage and screen depictions of the rock 'n' roll social dancing of the 1950s are probably no more authentic choreographically than those presented in the Hollywood films made during the 1950s. However, when the notion of dance "authenticity" is extended to include not just physical maneuvers, but the larger attitudes, energies, spirit, and cultural forces that underpin and are expressed through the dancing, then the later, nostalgic portrayals of the rock 'n' roll dancing of the 1950s may be considered reliable depictions.

As *Grease* was propelling the '50s nostalgia movement on stage and screen, music-industry producer Richard Nader furthered the '50s rock 'n' roll revival movement with the presentation of gigantic concert events at large-scale entertainment venues, such as New York's Madison Square Garden. Nader's shows featured famous musical artists from the 1950s performing their old hits. In 1973, Columbia Pictures released *Let the Good Times Roll*, a feature film documenting some of these musical events. Described in a press release as "a filmic concert" that jumps from past to present so time has no meaning and the viewer is being taken on a boundless memory trip, the movie intercut newsreel, film, and television clips from the 1950s with the

1970s concert footage.[18] The film garnered generally positive reviews from the critics, with *Women's Wear Daily* deeming it "one of the best documentaries ever made on culture."[19] It was effusively praised by a *New York Times* reviewer who wrote, "More than a nostalgic look at the great originators of rock 'n' roll, it evokes the real beginnings of the youth pop culture that blossomed in the sixties and caused so much social change."[20]

Let the Good Times Roll was photographed at two large concert events—one held in Detroit in April 1972 and the other at New York's Nassau Coliseum in May of that same year—and also includes footage from a Fats Domino show in Las Vegas. The film includes performances by Domino, Little Richard, Chuck Berry, Chubby Checker, Bill Haley and the Comets, Danny and the Juniors, several doo-wop groups, and others. While the artists' performances were irresistibly energizing and sparked lots of bopping around by the young audience members, some of the most entertaining parts of the movie are the vintage film clips, such as that of a group of teens sanding down the soles of their shoes to make for better Twisting, and a demonstration of what was considered proper, versus objectionable, school attire for '50s teens at Hicksville Junior High School on New York's Long Island.

While the use of the archival footage lent a playful, irreverent tone to the movie, much like that of a Sha-Na-Na performance, the film also exhibited strong 1970s sensibilities. Many of the concert performances were clearly influenced by developments that had occurred in rock music throughout the Sixties. Though they featured Fifties music, the concerts were obviously designed to appeal to the tastes of, and what was familiar to, the youth of the early Seventies. It was apparent that the performers were more concerned with playing to the audiences in front of them than with recreating the past. With the exception of the archival clips, *Let the Good Times Roll* is less valuable as historical documentation of the '50s and more important as a record of how the rock 'n' roll of that era was re-packaged to suit the sensibilities and fulfill the nostalgic interests of Seventies audiences.

The more important 1973 film, and a big boost to the era's '50s nostalgia movement, was *American Graffiti*, Hollywood's first rock 'n' roll blockbuster. Even though the movie was set in 1962, its soundtrack is a compilation of classic rock 'n' roll songs of the 1950s, a reflection of the period's "oldies but goodies" movement. Directed by George

Lucas, the plotless, atmospheric film about a group of cruising teen-agers uses the '50s rock hits to evoke a lost world of youthful inno-cence. "I wanted to preserve what a certain generation of Americans thought being a teenager was really about—from about 1945 to 1962," said Lucas.[21] The movie's soundtrack album became the most pop-ular collection of vintage '50s rock 'n' roll since Laboe's original "Oldies But Goodies," selling more than one million copies.[22] While most of the film's "choreography" is in the cruising movements of the cars, which "dance" a sort of motorized ballet, the movie does contain a scene at a sock hop in a school gymnasium and some footage of au-thentically recreated rock 'n' roll dances, most notably the Stroll.

It was the enormous popularity of *American Graffiti* that ultimately led television to join the rest of the entertainment industry in riding the early '70s wave of '50s nostalgia. On January 14, 1974, ABC pre-miered the situation comedy *Happy Days*, a show about a clean-cut high school guy and his pals, set in Milwaukee during the 1950s. The program's creator and executive producer Garry Marshall had been asked a few years earlier to create a show about young people that avoided the subject of drugs. But in light of the extensive role that drug use played in the lives of the youth of the early '70s, in order to comply with what he had been asked to do, Marshall decided to set his show in the 1950s. He also thought such a time shift might help the show attract contemporary viewers who, in his opinion, "were tired of the uncertainty of the '60s," and would like the innocence of that era.[23] A pilot of Marshall's show, then titled *New Family in Town*, was produced in 1971, but it was deemed too gentle, wholesome, and innocent, and was shelved. The pilot was recycled, re-titled to *Love and the Happy Days*, and aired in February 1972 on ABC's anthology series, *Love, American Style*. It is said that director George Lucas viewed the pilot to determine if its star, Ron Howard, would make a suitable early 1960s' teenager in his film *American Graffiti*.[24] As soon as *Ameri-can Graffiti* emerged as a hit movie, with Howard in the lead, Marshall was asked to re-try his '50s show and to maybe bring into the cast some characters from the wrong side of the tracks. It was then that the greaser Arthur Fonzarelli, affectionately known as "Fonzie," was added to the show and *Happy Days* went on to become a huge hit.[25]

Happy Days aired from 1974 to 1984, and spawned the spin-off *La-verne and Shirley*, an equally successful program, also set in the 1950s, which ran from 1976 to 1983. An animated version of *Happy Days* was broadcast on Saturday mornings from 1980 to 1983. Though as a non-musical, comedy series, the program featured no regular dance component and provides little in the way of historical documentation of period rock 'n' roll dancing, *Happy Days* constituted a major force in the Fifties nostalgia movement of the 1970s. The show was so popular that the character of Fonzie has become an American icon. His leather jacket is among the treasures housed in the Smithsonian National Museum of American History.

While the rage for '50s nostalgia began to wane at the end of the 1970s, for the next 30 years music, theater, film, and television producers continued to revisit the 1950s periodically, with concerts, shows, and movies of varying degrees of quality, popularity, and importance in terms of their depiction of the era's rock 'n' roll dancing. Least important dance-wise were the many bio-pics portraying the typically turbulent lives of the famous pioneers of rock 'n' roll music. The 1978 film *American Hot Wax* (harshly criticized for its overly reverential portrait of DJ Alan Freed) featured appearances by Chuck Berry and Jerry Lee Lewis, among others. Though it did include footage of Berry doing his duck walk and scenes depicting a Freed concert at the Brooklyn Paramount in which teens could be seen dancing in racially mixed couples, the movie includes no full-blown dance numbers. Released that same year, *The Buddy Holly Story* is also devoid of any dancing, other than some brief Jitterbugging clips. Based on the life of Ritchie Valens, the 1987 film *La Bamba* contains what appear to be authentically recreated Jitterbugging and slow dancing scenes, yet they constitute no more than a few seconds of screen time. A biography of Jerry Lee Lewis, the 1989 film *Great Balls of Fire!* choreographed by Bill and Jacqui Landrum, includes a scene in an African-American jook joint that shows some Bopping and two men dancing movements that resemble those of the Slop. The 2008 film *Cadillac Records* about Leonard Chess and the formation of his company, Chess Records, features no dancing whatsoever.

Though these bio-pics add little to the on-screen documentation of the social dancing of the 1950s, they do serve as important reminders of the centrality of movement to the performing styles of the early rock 'n' roll artists. The performances by the original artists in *American Hot Wax*, and the actors portraying the rock 'n' roll legends in the other films, compellingly illustrate the idiosyncratic movements adopted by these artists as they performed their trend-setting rock 'n' roll music.

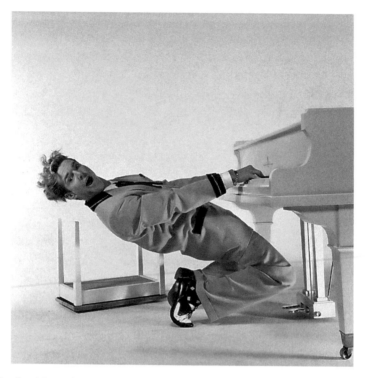

Dennis Quaid emphasizing the rock 'n' roll pioneer's unbridled movements in his depiction of Jerry Lee Lewis for the 1989 biopic *Great Balls of Fire!* (Orion Pictures/Photofest)

Perhaps the most valuable piece of cinematic '50s nostalgia, in terms of documentation of the era's rock 'n' roll dancing, is the 1988 John Waters film *Hairspray*. An offbeat satire, the movie features an extended ensemble sequence of teens dancing The Madison, clearly showing the basic step as well as many of the variations.

Because *Hairspray*'s story is set in 1962, its other dance numbers all reflect the social dancing of the early '60s. Yet the film's choreography vividly illuminates an important aspect of rock 'n' roll dancing common to both the '50s and the early '60s. As the film's storyline centers around a teenage girl's attempt to integrate the whites-only "Corny Collins Show," a television teen dance program modeled on Baltimore's *Buddy Deane Show*, the film's choreographer, Edward Love, drew upon his memories of the period dances he had watched his older sisters doing when he was a kid. Love also brought in one of the dancers who had appeared on *The Buddy Deane Show* to help him get the "right look." Love has described his choreography as "efficient in deciphering the stylistic differences between dancers from white and black neighborhoods" and it is in this regard that the film's dance numbers exhibit significant historical value. "The dancers on the 'Corny Collins Show' are white, and even though they do dances such as the Roach, which has black origins, there's no soul to it really. But the black dancers from the fringe neighborhoods doing the Slow Drag and Dirty Boogie really let loose. They didn't have to worry about looking pristine or avoiding the TV censors, since they weren't generally allowed to be on the show anyway," Love has said. Love has also pointed out that the dancing in the film "resists the temptation to be overly theatrical. It looks normal, not slick. . . . I would go home at the end of the day thinking [the dances] were going to look boring, but in the context of a live TV show, the dances are exactly right. The kids look authentic."[26]

When *Hairspray* was adapted into a Broadway musical in 2002, the stage production featured a Madison dance sequence, as in the movie. However, in 2007, the Broadway show was made into a movie musical, starring John Travolta, and for that film The Madison dance number was eliminated.

In 1990, Waters made another rock 'n' roll-oriented period film, *Cry-Baby*, which was set in 1954 and took a darkly satirical look at rockabilly music and its fans. In a grotesquely exaggerated depiction of the Baltimore teens who embraced the rockabilly genre, the film offers up dancing that is the complete opposite of the polished, theatricalized choreography often found in nostalgic '50s shows and movies. The dancers in *Cry-Baby* perform with a dorky awkwardness, clomping through basic Jitterbug moves with no sense of style, smoothness, or joy. While their skill level may have resembled that of many average '50s teens, their detached, draggy attitudes were more reflective of the film's parodic tone than of the kind of spirit or emotions likely to have been projected by actual teenagers as they danced in the '50s.

As Hollywood revisited the Fifties largely through bio-pics and satiric comedies, one of the methods by which Broadway continued to look back at the decade was also through biography. Based on the life of Buddy Holly, the 1990 Broadway musical *Buddy: The Buddy Holly Story* (which originated in London) contained virtually no on-stage choreography. However, the show's second act was a re-creation of the last concert Holly gave before his tragic death in the plane crash. Though surely inadvertently, the production generated dancing that replicated what had occurred at rock 'n' roll concerts in New York theaters in the 1950s. At the Broadway show's opening night performance, during the second-act "concert," audience members got out of their seats and danced in the theater aisles. As in the old days, structural engineers were called in to examine the theater building and deemed such dancing dangerous. From then on large signs had to be posted in the theater's mezzanine and balcony warning, "No Dancing" during the performance. In addition, the show's programs were stuffed with "No Dancing" notices, and the theater ushers were instructed to flash their lights at anyone seeming to have the urge to dance. If any audience members rose to dance, security officers were called in to stop them.[27]

The other primary manner in which Broadway continued to revisit the 1950s was through the creation of "jukebox musicals." A revue-like genre of musical theater, jukebox musicals use the body of work of a single composer, musical artist, or group to form the structure of a theatrical production that consists largely of musical numbers, usually tied together by a simple plot. A lively Fifties-oriented example of the genre is *All Shook Up*, a 2005 Broadway production based on the songs made famous by Elvis Presley. In order to create the show's authentic-feeling, albeit theatricalized, period dance numbers, its choreographer, Sergio Trujillo, did extensive preparatory research—studying '50s photographs, watching Hollywood films of the era, and examining clips from *American Bandstand*.[28]

Trujillo continued to draw upon that research for his choreography of the 2009 Broadway musical *Memphis*. A celebration of rock 'n' roll's roots in the "race music" of 1950s Memphis, the show won the Tony Award for Best Musical and is the most successful original, book-musical to revisit the Fifties since *Grease*. But Trujillo didn't want to be "a slave to the dance forms of the period," he explained. "I felt it was important for me to consider a younger audience and to make the choreography cool and hip and interesting and fresh for them. . . . What I tried to do was not to replicate what was done back then, but take all the information and come up with my own formula, my own vocabulary, which is a take on all the different dance styles of that time." Trujillo said that people who were around in the '50s would not recognize exact period dance steps in his *Memphis* choreography, but would certainly recognize the feel of the dancing.[29]

Yet while the show's choreography cannot be relied upon as strict documentation of Fifties dances, it does, in one number, demonstrate an elemental concept about the rhythm and blues music at the root of '50s rock 'n' roll: its irresistible power to make people dance. In a scene in a department store, in which a DJ is trying to convince the store owner that he can make more money by selling "race records," the DJ begins to play rhythm and blues recordings and mayhem ensues, as all the customers start dancing wildly to the music. In describing the choreography, Trujillo said, "Every customer in that department store had become so excited by the music—it took over their feet, their body, their legs—that they couldn't wait to buy the records."[30]

Right on the heels of the hit musical *Memphis* came the 2010 Broadway show *Million Dollar Quartet*, a jukebox musical that takes place on one day, December 4, 1956. On that day, at the Sun Records recording studio in downtown Memphis, Johnny Cash, Jerry Lee Lewis, Carl Perkins, and Elvis Presley gathered for an impromptu jam session. A re-creation of that historic event, the production contains no full-scale dance numbers. Yet the body movements of the four star performers, particularly those of Levi Kreis in his Tony Award-winning portrayal of Lewis, serve as reminders of the natural kinship that existed between movement and music in the performances of the pioneering rock 'n' roll artists.

After its big successes in the 1970s with *Happy Days* and *Laverne and Shirley*, television also continued to periodically revisit the 1950s. A 1994 cable-TV, partial re-make of the 1956 movie *Shake, Rattle and Rock* was insignificant dance-wise and, in all other respects, considered even worse than the original, sub-par '50s teen rock movie. However, in 2002 NBC premiered a nostalgic drama series, *American Dreams*, which revolved around the life of a teenage girl from Philadelphia, who was a regular dancer on *American Bandstand*. Though the series was set in the early 1960s, and its dances reflected that period, the importance of the *American Bandstand* program in the lives of the teens on the series was no different than it would have been for teens in the late 1950s. Notwithstanding Dick Clark's role as an executive producer of the series, the choice of the famous teen dance program to both symbolize the times and contextualize the series' exploration of the cultural, social, and political issues of the era is telling. It is yet further indication of how dynamically the rock 'n' roll dance floor can serve to illuminate many aspects of America's larger cultural climate.

By the end of the first decade of the 21st century, more than 50 years had passed since the birth of rock 'n' roll, and the youngsters who had grown up dancing to its earliest tunes were now in their sixties or early seventies. As it is that "older adult" demographic which is known to make up the bulk of public television viewers, as the 21st century settled in, '50s rock 'n' roll music programs began to spring up on PBS outlets nationwide. The nostalgic music programs quickly became a fund-raising staple and are broadcast in heavy doses whenever a station conducts a pledge drive.

Designed to exploit the nostalgic effects of hearing the music of their youth, which it is assumed will prompt viewers to tune in and donate money, the programs generally feature video-recordings of large concert events in which the original musical artists can be seen performing their greatest hits. While a performer such as Little Richard may appear from time to time, most of the featured artists are doo-wop groups, rather than the era's more raucous solo singers and instrumentalists. With the exception of some simplified choreography that the doo-wop groups sometimes offer, the programs generally include very little dancing due, one imagines, to the advanced ages of both the performers and the audience members shown seated at the concerts, most of whom look to be late middle-agers. Characterized by an abundance of the harmonious vocal groups, and an absence of any kind of vigorous dancing, these programs proffer an erroneous representation of the 1950s rock 'n' roll scene. While they do not always contain perfectly accurate historical recreations of the dancing of the period, and typically do not include performances by original Fifties artists, the nostalgic Broadway shows, Hollywood films, and commercial television programs may actually offer more valid replications of the rock 'n' roll music and dancing of the Fifties than do these PBS music specials.

Revisiting the Fifties Forever

Nostalgic journeys back to the 1950s via the era's rock 'n' roll music and dancing are likely to continue and perhaps even proliferate in years to come. The Fifties has become a fixture in feel-good nostalgia, as it seems to be the perfect decade to revisit in times of national stress, confusion, or cultural segmentation. It represents perhaps the last time in American history that a generation was held together by a popular music and dance culture that was common to a large percentage of its members. As rock 'n' roll music continued to evolve, it splintered into myriad sub-genres. And even though it exerted a pervasive influence on the pop music world at large, that musical scene has also become decidedly segmented. A signature feature of music radio in the early years of the 21st century was the introduction of a diverse selection of specialty stations. No matter how specific their musical preferences, listeners could likely find a radio station that would cater solely to their taste, be it country, rap, Broadway show tunes, Frank Sinatra recordings, or any one of a multitude of rock-oriented genres.

With its unprecedented size, the Baby Boomer generation, which came of age in the wake of rock 'n' roll's inception, has exerted a significant influence on the continuation of Fifties nostalgia. With their demands to hear the music of their youth and its forerunners, and to revel in memories associated with the popular culture of the times, performances of Fifties-style rock 'n' roll dancing may continue to re-surface for quite some time. But even as the Boomers recede into history, it is certain that future generations will face times of national discomfort or crises that will prompt yearnings for what is perceived to have been simpler, happier, or more harmonious eras. It is likely that Americans will want again and again to remember the Fifties, and the most visceral, affecting way to do so is through engagement with its popular music and dance.

Yet even though '50s rock 'n' roll can serve to return us to more comforting times, Sha-Na-Na member Richard Joffee argues that the impulse to revisit that music need not always be nostalgically inspired. Because the music was created out of and reflects a spirit of defiant rebellion, with its wild, movement-inducing rhythms, it will probably always appeal to generations or populations looking to instigate change or upheaval. "There is something innately revolutionary about energy," wrote Joffee.[31] Therefore, it is because of its dual nature—its power to both comfort and agitate—that 1950s rock 'n' roll music and the dancing it stimulates will always be with us.

Notes

Introduction

1. David Halberstam, *The Fifties* (New York: Random House, 1993), 244.
2. Ibid., 473, 474.
3. Ibid., 473–74.

Chapter 1

1. Alison Latham, ed., *The Oxford Companion to Music* (New York: Oxford University Press, 2002), 1275–76.
2. Joe Stuessy, *Rock and Roll: Its History and Stylistic Development* (Englewood Cliffs, NJ: Prentice Hall, 1990), 8, 19–20.
3. Charlie Gillett, *The Sound of the City: The Rise of Rock and Roll*, 2nd ed. (New York: Da Capo Press, 1996), 10.
4. Glenn C. Altschuler, *All Shook Up: How Rock 'n' Roll Changed America* (New York: Oxford University Press, 2003), 12.
5. Gillett, *The Sound of the City*, 21–22.
6. Stuessy, *Rock and Roll*, 78.
7. Gillett, *The Sound of the City*, 5.
8. Marc Fisher, *Something in the Air: Radio, Rock, and the Revolution That Shaped a Generation* (New York: Random House, 2007), 6.
9. Altschuler, *All Shook Up*, 33–34.
10. John A. Jackson, *Big Beat Heat: Alan Freed and the Early Years of Rock & Roll* (New York: Schirmer Books, MacMillan, 1991), 33.
11. James Miller, *Flowers in the Dustbin: The Rise of Rock and Roll, 1947–1977* (New York: Simon & Schuster, 1999), 35; and Gillett, *The Sound of the City*, 10.
12. Jackson, *Big Beat Heat*, 42.
13. Ibid., 62.
14. Ibid., 73–76.
15. Ibid., 80–83.
16. Miller, *Flowers in the Dustbin*, 102.

17. Peter Ford, "Rock Around the Clock and Me," www.peterford.com/ratc.html.

18. Jackson, *Big Beat Heat*, 120–21.

19. Ibid., 122.

20. Tami Stevens, email to author, April 1, 2010.

21. Halberstam, *The Fifties*, 300.

22. Ralph G. Giordano, *Social Dancing in America: A History and Reference*, vol. 2: *Lindy Hop to Hip Hop, 1901–2000* (Westport, CT: Greenwood Press, 2007), 138.

23. "100 Greatest Moments of the 20th Century," *George*, October 1999.

24. Jackson, *Big Beat Heat*, 142–43.

25. Mark Steyn, "The Man Who Invented Elvis," *Atlantic Monthly*, October 2003, 46.

26. Joe Levine, "Music Man," *TC Today: The Magazine of Teachers College, Columbia University*, Winter 2010, 19.

27. Jackson, *Big Beat Heat*, 140.

28. Ibid., 141.

29. John A. Jackson, *American Bandstand: Dick Clark and the Making of a Rock 'n' Roll Empire* (New York: Oxford University Press, 1997), 114.

30. Gillett, *The Sound of the City*, 92.

Chapter 2

1. Taken from commentary by the film's assistant director Joel Freeman, Peter Ford (son of the star Glenn Ford), and actors Jamie Farr and Paul Mazursky included on the Warner Home Video 2005 DVD of the 1955 MGM film *Blackboard Jungle*.

2. *Twist*, prod. and dir. Ron Mann, 78 min., Triton Pictures, 1993, documentary.

3. Jackson, *Big Beat Heat*, 92.

4. Anthony Macias, "Bringing Music to the People: Race, Urban Culture, and Municipal Politics in Postwar Los Angeles," *American Quarterly* 56, no. 3 (September 2004): 696–709.

5. Ray Smith, interview by author, tape recording, New York, N.Y., July 15, 2009.

6. Giordano, *Social Dancing in America*, 138.

7. Edith Evans Asbury, "Rock 'n' Roll Teen-Agers Tie Up the Times Square Area," *New York Times*, February 23, 1957.

8. Edith Evans Asbury, "Times Square 'Rocks' for Second Day," *New York Times*, February 24, 1957.

9. Giordano, *Social Dancing in America*, 140.

10. Jackson, *Big Beat Heat*, 98.

11. Giordano, *Social Dancing in America*, 140.

12. Jackson, *Big Beat Heat*, 98.

13. Ibid., 128–29.

14. Milton Bracker, "Experts Propose Study of 'Craze': Liken It to Medieval Lunacy, 'Contagious Dance Furies' and Bite of Tarantula," *New York Times*, February 23, 1957.

15. Jackson, *Big Beat Heat*, 86.

16. Ibid., 130.

17. Violet Sagolla, interview by author, Langhorne, Pa., January 19, 2010.

18. John W. Roberts, *From Hucklebuck to Hip-Hop: Social Dance in the African American Community in Philadelphia* (Philadelphia: Odunde, 1995), 12–13.

19. Benita Junette Brown, "Boppin' at Miss Mattie's Place: African-American Grassroots Dance Culture in North Philadelphia from the Speakeasy to the Uptown Theater During the 1960s" (Ph.D. diss., Temple University, 1999), 94, 115–16.

20. Roberts, *From Hucklebuck to Hip-Hop,* 35.

21. Marshall and Jean Stearns, *Jazz Dance: The Story of American Vernacular Dance* (New York: Schirmer Books, 1968), 12.

22. Jackson, *Big Beat Heat,* 97.

23. "Dancing: Program 3, Sex and Social Dance," prod. and dir. Ellen Hovde and Muffie Meyer, 58 min., Thirteen/WNET in assoc. with RM Arts and BBC-TV, 1993, documentary.

24. Katrina Hazzard-Gordon, *Jookin': The Rise of Social Dance Formations in African American Culture* (Philadelphia: Temple University Press, 1990), 79–82.

25. Dick Clark and Richard Robinson, *Rock, Roll and Remember* (New York: Popular Library, 1978), 147.

26. Richard M. Stephenson and Joseph Iaccarino, *The Complete Book of Ballroom Dancing* (New York: Doubleday, 1980), 42.

27. Karen Hubbard and Terry Monaghan, "Negotiating Compromise on a Burnished Wood Floor: Social Dancing at the Savoy," in *Ballroom, Boogie, Shimmy Sham, Shake: A Social and Popular Dance Reader,* ed. Julie Malnig (Urbana: University of Illinois Press, 2009), 145.

28. Advertisement for Samsung Jitterbug cell phone, *AARP Bulletin* 51, no. 3 (April 2010): 25.

29. *Arthur Murray Dance Lessons: Swing,* dir. Del Jack, 47 min., Pathe Pictures, Inc., 1990, instructional videotape.

30. Stevens, email to author.

31. Stephenson and Iaccarino, *The Complete Book of Ballroom Dancing,* 91.

32. Giordano, *Social Dancing in America,* 7–8, 151.

33. Lucius E. Lee, "Madison Dance Started in Columbus," *Ohio Sentinel,* 18 June 1960.

34. Charles Kelley, *The American Tap Dance Dictionary, Revised Edition* (New York: Dance Educators of America, 2002), 25, 76.

35. Albert and Josephine Butler, *Encyclopedia of Social Dance* (New York: Albert Butler Ballroom Dance Service, 1975), 242–44; *Twist,* video-recording; Giordano, *Social Dancing in America,* 151.

36. Tim Wall, "Rocking Around the Clock: Teenage Dance Fads from 1955 to 1965," in *Ballroom, Boogie, Shimmy Sham, Shake: A Social and Popular Dance Reader,* ed. Julie Malnig (Urbana: University of Illinois Press, 2009), 194.

Chapter 3

1. Clark and Robinson, *Rock, Roll and Remember,* 54.

2. "Filmusic Shorts for TV in Golden Sweep: 30G to 100G," *Billboard,* July 15, 1950, 7.

3. Otis L. Graham Jr. and Meghan Robinson Wander, eds., *Franklin D. Roosevelt: His Life and Times, An Encyclopedic View* (Boston: G. K. Hall, 1985), 370–71.

4. Clark and Robinson, *Rock, Roll and Remember,* 60.

5. Ibid., 62.

6. Pat Shook, interview by author, Penndel, Pa., May 18, 2010.

7. Smith, interview.

8. Clark and Robinson, *Rock, Roll and Remember,* 13, 96.

9. Shook, interview.

10. Clark and Robinson, *Rock, Roll and Remember,* 110; Altschuler, *All Shook Up,* 84.

11. Dick Clark, with Fred Bronson and captions by Ray Smith, *Dick Clark's American Bandstand* (New York: Collins, 1997), 50.

12. Arlene Sullivan, telephone conversation with author, July 28, 2009.

13. Smith, interview.

14. Clark, with Bronson and Smith, *Dick Clark's American Bandstand,* 49, 84.

15. Clark and Robinson, *Rock, Roll and Remember,* 107.

16. Julie Malnig, "Let's Go to the Hop: Community Values in Televised Teen Dance Programs of the Fifties and Early Sixties," in *Proceedings, Congress on Research in Dance Spring 2005 Conference: Dance and Community* (New York: The Print Center, 2005), 3, 5.

17. Jack Gunod, telephone conversation with author, August 22, 2009.

18. *Everybody Dance Now,* dir. and prod. Margaret Selby, 58 min., Thirteen/WNET, 1991, documentary on music videos.

19. Clark and Robinson, *Rock, Roll and Remember,* 180.

20. Smith, interview.

21. Sullivan, telephone conversation.

22. Clark, with Bronson and Smith, *Dick Clark's American Bandstand,* 64; Michael Shore, with Dick Clark, *The History of American Bandstand* (New York: Ballantine Books, 1985), 55; Jackson, *American Bandstand,* 20–21.

23. Jerry Blavat, telephone conversation with author, January 8, 2010.

24. Smith, interview.

25. Malnig, "Let's Go to the Hop," 6–7; Roberts, *From Hucklebuck to Hip-Hop,* 35; Brown, "Boppin' at Miss Mattie's Place," 51; Smith, interview.

26. Roberts, *From Hucklebuck to Hip-Hop,* 35.

27. *Twist,* documentary.

28. Sharon Decker, interview by author, Penndel, Pa, May 18, 2010.

29. Shore, with Clark, *The History of American Bandstand,* 74.

30. Ibid., 91–92.

31. Clark and Robinson, *Rock, Roll and Remember,* 132.

32. Ibid., 227.

33. Brown, "Boppin' at Miss Mattie's Place," 135–36.

34. Sharon Decker, interview.

35. Brown, "Boppin' at Miss Mattie's Place," 134.

36. Johnny Sands, *How to Bop* (Santa Monica, CA: DSJ, 1955); Art Silva, *How to Dance the Bop!* (Hollywood: Self-published pamphlet, 1956).

37. Clark and Robinson, *Rock, Roll and Remember,* 136.

38. Jackson, *American Bandstand,* 211.

39. Blavat, telephone conversation; Roberts, *From Hucklebuck to Hip-Hop,* 97.

40. Gillett, *The Sound of the City,* 135.

41. Roberts, *From Hucklebuck to Hip-Hop,* 84–85.

42. Sullivan, telephone conversation.

43. Clark and Robinson, *Rock, Roll and Remember,* 224.

44. Dorothea Duryea Ohl, "Hawaiian Rock 'n' Roll," *Dance Magazine,* March 1958, 78.

45. Sullivan, telephone conversation.

46. Jackson, *American Bandstand,* 12.

47. Malnig, "Let's Go to the Hop," 2.

48. Dan Dillon, *So, Where'd You Go to High School: The Baby Boomer Edition* (St. Louis: Virginia Publishing Company, 2005), 226; Malnig, "Let's Go to the Hop," 3–4; Giordano, *Social Dancing in America,*149–50.

49. Malnig, "Let's Go to the Hop," 9.

50. Jackson, *Big Beat Heat,* 168.

Chapter 4

1. Geoffrey Holder, "Not to Twist," *Ebony,* February 1962, 107.

2. Jim Dawson, *The Twist: The Story of the Song and Dance That Changed the World* (Boston: Faber & Faber, 1995), 35.

3. Dawson, *The Twist,* 131.

4. Clark and Robinson, *Rock, Roll and Remember,* 140.

5. Holder, "Not to Twist," 107.

6. Gillett, *The Sound of the City,* 206.

7. Smith, interview.

8. Shore, with Clark, *The History of American Bandstand,* 24.

9. Clark, with Bronson and Smith, *Dick Clark's American Bandstand,* 17.

10. Miller, *Flowers in the Dustbin,* 148.

11. Altschuler, *All Shook Up,* 85.

12. Stuessy, *Rock and Roll,* 85.

13. "State Curb Asked on Dance Studios," *New York Times,* February 22, 1958, 8.

14. "Ethics Code Signed by 3 Dance Studios After State Inquiry," *New York Times,* October 15, 1959, 47.

15. "Dancing Studios Face Coast Study," *New York Times,* October 1, 1962, 35.

16. Halberstam, *The Fifties,* 664.

17. Jackson, *Big Beat Heat,* 240.

18. William M. Blair, "Wider TV Inquiry to Study Bribery and Paid 'Plugs,'" *New York Times,* November 7, 1959, 13.

19. Jackson, *Big Beat Heat,* 294.

20. Ibid., 245.

21. Jackson, *American Bandstand,* 194.

22. Gillett, *The Sound of the City,* 206.

23. Dawson, *The Twist,* xi–xii.

24. Jackson, *American Bandstand,* 212.

25. *Twist,* documentary.

26. Dawson, *The Twist,* 16.

27. *Twist,* documentary.

28. Clark and Robinson, *Rock, Roll and Remember,* 138.

29. Dawson, *The Twist,* 27.

30. Clark and Robinson, *Rock, Roll and Remember,* 138.

31. *Twist,* documentary.

32. Dawson, *The Twist*, 34.

33. *Best of Bandstand*, prod., Paul Brownstein, 47 min., Vestron Music Video, 1986, compilation of kinescopes from the television show *American Bandstand* dating from 1957 to 1960.

34. Smith, interview.

35. Ibid.

36. Blavat, telephone conversation.

37. *Twist*, documentary.

38. Ibid.

39. Stearns and Stearns, *Jazz Dance*, 4.

40. Ibid., 1.

41. Ibid., 122.

42. Ibid., 107.

43. Ibid., 98–99.

44. Dawson, *The Twist*, 2.

45. Ibid., 48–51.

46. *The Twist*, documentary.

47. Arthur Gelb, "Habitues of Meyer Davis Land Dance the Twist," *New York Times*, October 19, 1961, 37.

48. *Twist*, documentary.

49. Dawson, *The Twist*, 55–56.

50. Ibid., 59.

51. Ibid., 65.

52. Ibid., 58.

53. Ibid., 60.

54. Carl Belz, *The Story of Rock*, 2nd ed. (New York: Oxford University Press, 1972), 91.

55. *Swing, Bop, and Hand Dance*, prod. Beverly Lindsay, dir. Bill Pratt, 45 min., WHMM-TV, Howard University, 1997, documentary.

56. Al Decker, interview by author, Penndel, Pa., May 18, 2010.

57. Sullivan, phone conversation; Nancy Finnegan, telephone conversation with author, August 22, 2009.

58. Gunod, telephone conversation.

59. Belz, *The Story of Rock*, 214.

60. Ibid., 84.

Chapter 5

1. Halberstam, *The Fifties*, 514.

2. Miller, *Flowers in the Dustbin*, 312–13.

3. Stephen Holden, "Sha Na Na Revisits the 50's and 60's," *New York Times*, March 13, 1981, C17.

4. David P. Szatmary, *Rockin' in Time: A Social History of Rock and Roll* (Englewood Cliffs, NJ: Prentice-Hall, 1987), 170.

5. Annie Fisher, "Sha-Na-Yeah!," *Village Voice*, July 3, 1969; Sha-Na-Na press release, in Sha-Na-Na (musical group) clippings file, Music Division, New York Public Library for the Performing Arts.

6. Don Heckman, "Cheech and Chong Show Comedic Skill on Sha-Na-Na Bill," *New York Times*, December 30, 1971.

7. Fisher, "Sha-Na-Yeah!"

8. Belz, *The Story of Rock*, 212–13.

9. "Racial Incident Marks Sha Na Na S. Africa Gig," *Billboard*, May 28, 1983, 59.

10. Richard Joffee, "Is Rock 'n' Roll *Really* Here to Stay?," *Village Voice*, June 14, 1973, 52.

11. Craig Evans, email to author, September 4, 2010.

12. Joffee, "Is Rock 'n' Roll *Really* Here to Stay?" 52.

13. Randall Poe, "The '50s Are No. 1," *Daily News*, December 2, 1979, Leisure, 5.

14. J. Hoberman, "Film: Quintet," *Village Voice*, June 29, 1982, 66.

15. John Lahr, "The Theatre: Can't Stop the Beat," *New Yorker*, October 26, 2009, 96.

16. Nan Robertson, "Champion's Challenge," *New York Times*, April 10, 1960.

17. Ibid.

18. "Production Notes: *Let the Good Times Roll*," *News*, Columbia Pictures, May 5, 1973.

19. Daphne Davis, "Let the Good Times Roll," *Women's Wear Daily*, May 24, 1973.

20. Loraine Alterman, "Yes, Rock Can Sometimes Save a Bad Movie," *New York Times*, July 8, 1973, 8, 19.

21. Miller, *Flowers in the Dustbin*, 312.

22. Ibid., 316–17.

23. Gary Marshall, "Happy Days," *TV Guide*, February 29, 1992.

24. "Happy Days," www.tv.com.

25. Marshall, "Happy Days."

26. Kevin Grubb, "Broadway and Beyond: Putting the Bounce in *Hairspray's* Dances," *Dance Magazine*, June 1988, 62.

27. Alex Witchel, "On Stage, and Off," *New York Times*, November 23, 1990.

28. Lisa Jo Sagolla, "Capturing the Feel of 1950s Memphis," *Back Stage*, November 19–25, 2009, 12.

29. Ibid.

30. Ibid.

31. Joffee, "Is Rock 'n' Roll *Really* Here to Stay?," 52.

Bibliography

Books and Articles

Alterman, Loraine. "Yes, Rock Can Sometimes Save a Bad Movie." *New York Times*, July 8, 1973, 8, 19.

Altschuler, Glenn C. *All Shook Up: How Rock 'n' Roll Changed America*. New York: Oxford University Press, 2003.

Asbury, Edith Evans. "Rock 'n' Roll Teen-Agers Tie Up the Times Square Area." *New York Times*, February 23, 1957, 1, 12.

Asbury, Edith Evans. "Times Square 'Rocks' for Second Day." *New York Times*, February 24, 1957, 37.

Belz, Carl. *The Story of Rock*. 2nd ed. New York: Oxford University Press, 1972.

Blair, William M. "Wider TV Inquiry to Study Bribery and Paid 'Plugs,'" *New York Times*, November 7, 1959, 1, 13.

Bracker, Milton. "Experts Propose Study of 'Craze': Liken It to Medieval Lunacy, 'Contagious Dance Furies' and Bite of Tarantula." *New York Times*, February 23, 1957, 12.

Brown, Benita Junette. "Boppin' at Miss Mattie's Place: African-American Grassroots Dance Culture in North Philadelphia from the Speakeasy to the Uptown Theater during the 1960s." Ph.D. diss., Temple University, 1999.

Butler, Albert, and Josephine Butler. *Encyclopedia of Social Dance*. New York: Albert Butler Ballroom Dance Service, 1975.

Clark, Dick, with Fred Bronson and captions by Ray Smith. *Dick Clark's American Bandstand*. New York: Collins, 1997.

Clark, Dick, and Richard Robinson. *Rock, Roll and Remember*. New York: Popular Library, 1978.

"Dancing Studios Face Coast Study." *New York Times*, October 1, 1962, 35.

Davis, Daphne. "Let the Good Times Roll." *Women's Wear Daily*, May 24, 1973.

Dawson, Jim. *The Twist: The Story of the Song and Dance That Changed the World*. Boston: Faber & Faber, 1995.

Dillon, Dan. *So, Where'd You Go to High School: The Baby Boomer Edition*. St. Louis: Virginia Publishing, 2005.

"Ethics Code Signed by 3 Dance Studios after State Inquiry." *New York Times*, October 15, 1959, 47.

"Filmusic Shorts for TV in Golden Sweep: 30G to 100G." *Billboard*, July 15, 1950, 7.

Fisher, Annie. "Sha-Na-Yeah!" *Village Voice*, July 3, 1969.

Fisher, Marc. *Something in the Air: Radio, Rock, and the Revolution That Shaped a Generation*. New York: Random House, 2007.

Gelb, Arthur. "Habitues of Meyer Davis Land Dance the Twist." *New York Times*, October 19, 1961, 37, 39.

Gillett, Charlie. *The Sound of the City: The Rise of Rock and Roll*. 2nd ed. New York: Da Capo Press, 1996.

Gilvey, John Anthony. *Before the Parade Passes By: Gower Champion and the Glorious American Musical*. New York: St. Martin's Press, 2005.

Giordano, Ralph G. *Social Dancing in America: A History and Reference*. Vol. 2, *Lindy Hop to Hip Hop, 1901–2000*. Westport, CT: Greenwood Press, 2007.

Gould, Jack. "TV: New Phenomenon; Elvis Presley Rises to Fame as Vocalist Who Is Virtuoso of Hootchy-Kootchy." *New York Times*, June 6, 1956.

Graham, Otis L., Jr., and Meghan Robinson Wander, eds. *Franklin D. Roosevelt: His Life and Times, an Encyclopedic View*. Boston: G. K. Hall, 1985.

Grubb, Kevin. "Broadway and Beyond: Putting the Bounce in *Hairspray*'s Dances." *Dance Magazine*, June 1988, 62.

Halberstam, David. *The Fifties*. New York: Random House, 1993.

Hammond, John. "New Dance Fad: The Rock 'n' Roll." *New York Herald-Tribune*, July 18, 1955.

Hazzard-Gordon, Katrina. *Jookin': The Rise of Social Dance Formations in African American Culture*. Philadelphia: Temple University Press, 1990.

Heckman, Don. "Cheech and Chong Show Comedic Skill on Sha-Na-Na Bill." *New York Times*, December 30, 1971.

Hoberman, J. "Film: Quintet." *Village Voice*, June 29, 1982, 66.

Holden, Stephen. "Sha Na Na Revisits the 50's and 60's." *New York Times*, March 13, 1981, C17.

Holder, Geoffrey. "Not to Twist." *Ebony*, February 1962, 107.

Hubbard, Karen, and Terry Monaghan. "Negotiating Compromise on a Burnished Wood Floor: Social Dancing at the Savoy." In *Ballroom, Boogie, Shimmy Sham, Shake: A Social and Popular Dance Reader*, edited by Julie Malnig, 126–45. Urbana: University of Illinois Press, 2009.

Hunter, Evan. *The Blackboard Jungle*. 50th anniversary ed. New York: Pocket Books, 2004.

Jackson, John A. *American Bandstand: Dick Clark and the Making of a Rock 'n' Roll Empire*. New York: Oxford University Press, 1997.

Jackson, John A. *Big Beat Heat: Alan Freed and the Early Years of Rock & Roll*. New York: Schirmer Books, 1991.

Joffee, Richard. "Is Rock 'n' Roll *Really* Here to Stay?" *Village Voice*, June 14, 1973, 52.

Kelley, Charles. *The American Tap Dance Dictionary*. Rev. ed. New York: Dance Educators of America, 2002.

Lahr, John. "The Theatre: Can't Stop the Beat." *New Yorker*, October 26, 2009, 96–97.

Latham, Alison, ed. *The Oxford Companion to Music*. New York: Oxford University Press, 2002.

Lee, Lucius E. "Madison Dance Started in Columbus." *Ohio Sentinel*, June 18, 1960. Accessed on ColumbusMusicHistory.com.

Levine, Joe. "Music Man." *TC Today: The Magazine of Teachers College, Columbia University*, Winter 2010, 18–19.

Lounsbury, Jim. *Hey, Look—I'm on TV: Chicago Television and Rock 'n' Roll, the Early Years*. Tucson: Jim Lounsbury Enterprises, 2000.

Macías, Anthony. "Bringing Music to the People: Race, Urban Culture, and Municipal Politics in Postwar Los Angeles." *American Quarterly* 56, no. 3 (September 2004): 693–717.

Malnig, Julie. *Ballroom, Boogie, Shimmy Sham, Shake: A Social and Popular Dance Reader*. Urbana: University of Illinois Press, 2009.

Malnig, Julie. "Let's Go to the Hop: Community Values in Televised Teen Dance Programs of the Fifties and Early Sixties." In *Proceedings, Congress on Research in Dance Spring 2005 Conference: Dance and Community*. New York: The Print Center, 2005.

Marshall, Garry. "Happy Days." *TV Guide*, February 29, 1992.

Miller, James. *Flowers in the Dustbin: The Rise of Rock and Roll, 1947–1977*. New York: Simon & Schuster, 1999.

Ohl, Dorothea Duryea. "Hawaiian Rock 'n' Roll." *Dance Magazine*, March 1958, 78.

"100 Greatest Moments of the 20th Century." *George*, October 1999.

Poe, Randall. "The '50s Are No. 1." *Daily News*, December 2, 1979, Leisure sec., 1, 5.

"Racial Incident Marks Sha Na Na S. Africa Gig." *Billboard*, May 28, 1983, 59.

Roberts, John. W. *From Hucklebuck to Hip-Hop: Social Dance in the African American Community in Philadelphia*. Philadelphia: Odunde, 1995.

Robertson, Nan. "Champion's Challenge." *New York Times*, April 10, 1960.

Sagolla, Lisa Jo. "Capturing the Feel of 1950s Memphis." *Back Stage*, November 19–25, 2009, 12.

Sands, Johnny. *How to Bop*. Santa Monica, CA: DSJ, 1955.

Shore, Michael, with Dick Clark. *The History of American Bandstand*. New York: Ballantine Books, 1985.

Silva, Art. *How to Dance the Bop!* Hollywood: Self-published pamphlet, 1956.

"State Curb Asked on Dance Studios." *New York Times*, February 22, 1958, 8.

Stearns, Marshall, and Jean Stearns. *Jazz Dance: The Story of American Vernacular Dance*. New York: Schirmer Books, 1968.

Stephenson, Richard M., and Joseph Iaccarino. *The Complete Book of Ballroom Dancing*. New York: Doubleday, 1980.

Steyn, Mark. "The Man Who Invented Elvis: Sam Phillips (1923–2003)." *Atlantic Monthly*, October 2003, 44–46.

Stuessy, Joe. *Rock and Roll: Its History and Stylistic Development*. Englewood Cliffs, NJ: Prentice Hall, 1990.

Szatmary, David P. *Rockin' in Time: A Social History of Rock and Roll*. Englewood Cliffs, NJ: Prentice-Hall, 1987.

Wall, Tim. "Rocking Around the Clock: Teenage Dance Fads from 1955 to 1965." In *Ballroom, Boogie, Shimmy Sham, Shake: A Social and Popular Dance Reader*, edited by Julie Malnig, 182–98. Urbana: University of Illinois Press, 2009.

Witchel, Alex. "On Stage and Off." *New York Times*, November 23, 1990.

Hollywood Films

American Graffiti. 110 min. Universal Pictures, 1973.

American Hot Wax. 91 min. Paramount Pictures, 1978.

Blackboard Jungle. 101 min. MGM, 1955. Released on DVD by Warner Home Video in 2005.
The Buddy Holly Story. 113 min. Columbia Pictures, 1978.
Bye Bye Birdie. 112 min. Columbia Pictures, 1963.
Cadillac Records. 108 min. TriStar Pictures, 2008.
Don't Knock the Rock. 84 min. Columbia Pictures, 1956.
Don't Knock the Twist. 87 min. Columbia Pictures, 1962.
Flaming Star. 91 min. 20th Century Fox, 1960.
G.I. Blues. 104 min., Paramount Pictures, 1960.
The Girl Can't Help It. 99 min. 20th Century Fox, 1956.
Go, Johnny, Go! 75 min. Hal Roach Studios, 1959.
Grease. 110 min. Paramount Pictures, 1978.
Great Balls of Fire! 102 min. Orion Pictures, 1989.
Hairspray. 96 min. New Line Cinema. 1988.
Hairspray. 115 min. New Line Cinema, 2007.
Hey, Let's Twist! 80 min. Paramount Pictures, 1961.
Jailhouse Rock. 96 min. MGM, 1957.
Jamboree! 71 min. Warner Brothers, 1957.
King Creole. 116 min. Paramount Pictures, 1958.
La Bamba. 108 min. Columbia Pictures, 1987.
Let the Good Times Roll. 98 min. Columbia Pictures, 1973.
Love Me Tender. 89 min. 20th Century Fox, 1956.
Loving You. 101 min. Paramount Pictures, 1957.
Mr. Rock and Roll. 86 min. Paramount Pictures, 1957.
Rock, Rock, Rock! 83 min. Vanguard Productions, 1956.
Rock Around the Clock. 77 min. Columbia Pictures, 1956.
Shake, Rattle and Rock. 72 min. Sunset Productions, 1956.
Twist All Night. 78 min. Keelou Corporation, 1961.
Twist Around the Clock. 86 min. Columbia Pictures, 1961.

Documentaries and Archival Video-Recordings

Alan Freed's Big Beat & Studio Party, ca. 1957, WABD-Dumont, New York City, approx. 55 min., Video Resources New York, Inc.
Arthur Murray Dance Lessons: Swing, dir. Del Jack, 47 min., Pathe Pictures, Inc., 1990.
Bandstand Days, 59 min., Teleduction, Inc., Washington, D.C., 1997.
Best of Bandstand, prod. Paul Brownstein, 47 min., Vestron Music Video, 1986.
Dancing: Program 3, Sex and Social Dance, prod. and dir. Ellen Hovde and Muffie Meyer, 58 min., Thirteen/WNET in association with RM Arts and BBC-TV, 1993.
Elvis: The Ed Sullivan Show—The Classic Performances, exec. prod. Andrew Holt, 47 min., Image Entertainment, 2009.
Everybody Dance Now, dir. and prod. Margaret Selby, 58 min., Thirteen/WNET, 1991.
1950s Teen Dance TV Shows, vol. 1, *The Video Beat: 1950s & 1960s Rock 'n' Roll on Video.*
1950s Teen Dance TV Shows, vol. 2, *The Video Beat: 1950s & 1960s Rock 'n' Roll on Video.*

Swing, Bop, and Hand Dance, prod. Beverly Lindsay, dir. Bill Pratt, 45 min., WHMM-TV, Howard University, 1997.
Twist, prod. and dir. Ron Mann, 78 min., Triton Pictures, 1993.

Personal Interviews and Correspondence

Jerry Blavat, telephone conversation with author, January 8, 2010.
Al Decker, interview by author, Penndel, PA, May 18, 2010.
Sharon Decker, interview by author, Penndel, PA, May 18, 2010.
Craig Evans, email to author, September 4, 2010.
Nancy Finnegan, telephone conversation with author, August 22, 2009.
Jack Gunod, telephone conversation with author, August 22, 2009.
Violet Sagolla, interview by author, Langhorne, PA, January 19, 2010.
Pat Shook, interview by author, Penndel, PA, May 18, 2010.
Ray Smith, interview by author, tape recording, New York, NY, July 15, 2009.
Tami Stevens, email to author, April 1, 2010.
Arlene Sullivan, telephone conversation with author, July 28, 2009.

Miscellaneous Materials

Advertisement for Samsung Jitterbug cell phone. *AARP Bulletin* 51, no. 3 (April 2010): 25.
"Production Notes: *Let the Good Times Roll*." *News*, Columbia Pictures, May 5, 1973. In *Let the Good Times Roll* (cinema, 1973) clippings file, Billy Rose Theatre Division, New York Public Library for the Performing Arts.
Sha-Na-Na press release, in Sha-Na-Na (Musical group) clippings file, Music Division, New York Public Library for the Performing Arts.

Internet Sources

Ford, Peter. "Rock Around the Clock and Me." www.peterford.com/ratc.html.
"Happy Days." www.tv.com.

Index

African Americans, 55; and *American Bandstand*, 63–64, 69; and American vernacular dances, 35–37, 65–67, 90; jook joints, 38; migration north, 6; and rhythm and blues, 2–3, 6; rock 'n' roll dances, influences on, 35–37, 47–48, 62–64, 67, 69–70, 86–87, 113; and rock 'n' roll music, 78; and television teen dance shows, 63–64, 67, 70, 74

African dance, 36–37

"Ain't That a Shame" (song), 8, 15

Alabama White Citizens Council, 34

Allen, Steve, 21

All Shook Up (Broadway musical), 114

Altman, Robert, 43

American Bandstand (television show), 30, 36, 50, 51, 114, 115; camera work, 64–65; dance contests, 57, 71; dress code, 59; history of, 51–57; and music videos, 60; as reality TV, 60–61; Record Review (Rate-a-Record), 57–58; rock 'n' roll dances, influence on, 57, 62–72, 86–89; rock 'n' roll music, influence on, 57, 61, 65, 71, 78–80; teenage dancers appearing on, 54–60, 62–65, 72; teenagers, influence on, 56–57, 58, 59–60, 64–65; and teen idols, 78–80; See also *Bandstand*

American Dreams (television show), 115

American Graffiti (film), 40, 69, 109–10

American Hot Wax (film), 111

"American Pie" (song), 80

American Society of Composers, Authors, and Publishers (ASCAP), 4, 5, 6, 84

Anka, Paul, 79

Ann-Margret, 107

Anthony, Ray, 62

Appell, Dave, and the Applejacks, 71

Arden, Eve, 106

Arthur Murray Dance Studios, 81, 90

Art Laboe Show, The (television show), 74

ASCAP. *See* American Society of Composers, Authors, and Publishers

Atlanta, 30

Atlantic City, 48

"At the Hop" (song), 65

Avallone, Francis Thomas (Frankie Avalon), 16, 79

Avalon, Frankie. *See* Avallone, Francis Thomas

Baby Boomers, 117

Ballard, Hank, 86–90

Ballard, Jovada and Jimmy, 14

"Ballin' the Jack" (song), 90

About the Author

Lisa Jo Sagolla is the author of *The Girl Who Fell Down: A Biography of Joan McCracken*. She is a columnist and critic for *Back Stage* and the *Kansas City Star* and has written extensively on dance, theater, and film for scholarly journals and encyclopedias. Sagolla teaches at Columbia University and works as an educational consultant for K–12 arts programs. She has also choreographed more than 75 Off-Broadway, regional, summer stock, and university productions. Sagolla holds an Ed.D. from Columbia University's Teachers College.